GRASS ROOTS AND GLASS CEILINGS

AFRICAN AMERICAN ADMINISTRATORS
IN
PREDOMINANTLY WHITE COLLEGES
AND
UNIVERSITIES

Edited by
WILLIAM B. HARVEY

State University of New York Press

Published by
State University of New York Press, Albany

© 1999 State University of New York

Printed in the United States of America

For information, address State University of New York Press,
State University Plaza, Albany, N.Y., 12246

Production by Marilyn P. Semerad
Marketing by Patrick Durocher

Library of Congress Cataloging-in-Publication Data

Grass roots and glass ceilings : African American administrators in
  predominantly white colleges and universities / edited by William B.
  Harvey.
      p.   cm. — (SUNY series, frontiers in education)
    Includes bibliographical references and index.
      ISBN 0-7914-4163-6 (hardcover : alk. paper). — ISBN 0-7914-4164-4
  (pbk. : alk. paper)
      1. Discrimination in higher education—United States.   2. Afro
  —American college administrators.   I. Harvey, William B. (William
  Bernard)   II. Series.
    LC212.42.G73   1999
    378.1'11'08996073—dc21   98-46464
                                                                  CIP

10 9 8 7 6 5 4 3 2 1

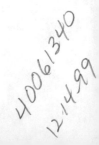

To the Harvey women:

My mother,
Mildred Delores Harvey

My wife,
Brenda Nichols Harvey

My daughters,
Adia Mandisa Harvey
Amina Tabia Harvey

Contents

Introduction

WILLIAM B. HARVEY

The Climb to the Top

Though countless leadership studies and analyses have been conducted over the years, the manner in which individuals move to the top levels of their units or organizations still cannot be explained in a specific, precise fashion. In institutions of higher education, unlike most business, political, military, or religious institutions, the selection process includes a significant degree of involvement by colleagues in the "search" that is being conducted. For most individuals who hold administrative positions in colleges and universities, particularly at the level of dean or higher, the review of the candidates includes an assessment of their qualifications and accomplishments to determine that they have not only the appropriate academic background and professional preparation, but also the personal style and mannerisms to carry out the designated job responsibilities in an effective manner.

While the personal qualities that help to propel some individuals, but not others, into top administrative positions cannot be easily delineated, there are some immutable characteristics that have been responsible for persons who have the requisite qualifications nevertheless being ruled out of consideration for particular positions in certain types of institutions. The most obvious such characteristic in America's colleges and universities has been race—the history and legacy of racial discrimination in America has meant that, except in very isolated situations, African Americans have not received equal consideration for positions, especially positions of power and authority, in the predominantly white colleges and universities.

In the three decades during which predominantly white institutions of higher education have been desegregated, some important gains have been made, although in regards to matters of race, serious problems and difficulties continue to exist. One important index of progress is the elevation of African Americans to significant positions within the hierarchy of the administrative structures at predominantly white colleges and universities. These advances, however, must be assessed in relation to the continued prevalence of racism in institutions of higher education, the significant underrepresentation of African Americans in administrative and faculty positions, and the existence of a foreboding social climate that encourages resistance to efforts and actions that are intended to expand affirmative action and multicultural representation.

In this volume, African Americans who currently hold or have previously held senior-level administrative positions (deans, vice-presidents, and presidents) in predominantly white colleges and universities present their views regarding academic culture and practice. These persons are members of a very small cohort, and even though they have achieved a high level of professional success, none of them has been insulated from the indignities of racism as their careers have unfolded. By sharing information about their career paths and personal experiences, the contributors highlight some of the significant anomalies within the higher education arena, explore patterns of interaction and behavior in the predominantly white colleges and universities, and reveal some of the values and attitudes that manifest themselves in these institutions.

The insights provided by senior African American administrators help to provide greater clarity about ways in which educational, social, and political issues, including race relations, are reflected in predominantly white colleges and universities. By virtue of their exemplary records and accomplishments, the contributors can be said, by any fair and reasonable analysis, to have surmounted successfully the negative stereotypes that are frequently applied to African Americans. These are not the whiny musings of "wannabees" or the self-serving exaggerations of "couldabeens"—they are the poignant reflections of men and women who have climbed their way to the top, but who have not forgotten what it is like to be on the bottom.

The Academic Climate

Observers of the academic environment would likely regard it as a placid, perhaps even serene setting, where the highly educated members of an esteemed profession engage in various activities which lead to the greater enlightenment of the next generation. While some elements of this presentation are accurate, in the predominately white colleges and universities, this general atmosphere of serenity has been less accessible for African Americans than for their white counterparts. The basis for identifying and advancing individuals who carry out administrative responsibilities in institutions of higher education is ostensibly based on intellect, performance, and capability. However, as indicated by the contributions to this volume, racial considerations often emerge as individual actions, institutional policies, or both. Depending on the timing and the callousness of the specific occurrence, African American administrators may be frustrated, discouraged, enraged, or merely embarrassed by specific situations that occur in the institutions where they carry out their duties and functions.

By and large, the culture of higher education has not been proactive or energetic in terms of identifying, advancing, and supporting African Americans who aspire to positions of leadership. Indeed, protracted resistance to affirmative action policies and practices which promote diversity in higher education has resulted in sparse representation of African Americans at senior administrative levels. Certainly, there is no shortage of willing, well-prepared candidates. The paucity of African Americans and the continued overrepresentation of white males in leadership positions have not diminished the fervor with which opponents of diversity have attacked the existence of programs that are intended to bring about a greater degree of racial balance in predominantly white institutions. In colleges and universities, settings where the celebration of the intellect might suggest that the power of reason would transcend the power of prejudice, the insidious presence of racism and discrimination is felt, just as it is in other social institutions. Thus, the success of African American administrators and their elevation to high-level positions in these settings remain rare occurrences. When such a situation does occur, it can usually be said to have taken place, not because of the system, but in spite of it.

Perseverance and Performance

While African Americans aspire to the highest level administrative positions just as their white counterparts do, placement patterns indicate that the areas in which they tend to find greater representation are also the sectors of the institution that are less often regarded as pathways to the top. For example, within the administrative arena, a greater proportion of African Americans seem to be located within the student affairs, minority affairs, and affirmative action arenas than are found in academic affairs or financial affairs. While there may be deanships and vice-presidencies within these areas that can be accessed by persons who move up through the ranks of these institutional categories, the conventional wisdom regarding movement into presidencies and chancellorships suggests that such actions are much less likely to occur for individuals who are not within the academic or financial affairs areas. There are exceptions to this "rule," even among African American administrators, which could be taken as an indication that extraordinary situations do occasionally occur, and, in rare cases, it is possible to surmount the barriers that are presented, no matter how high or wide they may be. Still, successful African American administrators, even those who reach the highest level at their particular institutions, invariably have to endure and overcome personal slights, insults, aggravations, and annoyances that are directed at them solely because of their color. While it might be presumed that any dedicated professional who is attempting to advance in his or her field would demonstrate a high level of perseverance, this particular quality would seem to take on special significance when one considers that, whatever the quality of performance that one might deliver, race is likely to be a factor in the way that one is viewed, and perhaps even judged.

How then, do African American administrators make it to the top rungs of predominately white institutions? The individual stories of accomplishment that follow are as different as the persons that they represent. There are some common qualities that can be ascribed to the members of this cohort—outstanding performance and dogged perseverance have already been mentioned, but high self-esteem, vision, leadership, and integrity are among the other very evident characteristics. Even with these qualities, and the inestimable value of a good network of contacts and associates, the intangibles of timing and just plain good luck also factor into the equation. The representations in this volume are instructive because they tell us how far we have come and, equally important, how far we have to go.

Predominantly white colleges and universities frequently describe or present themselves as places that are sensitive to and concerned about affirmative action and diversity. The contributors to this volume describe racist situations that they have faced in various kinds of institutions—large and small, public and private, urban and rural—in locations that range from New England to the heartland of middle America, and from the West Coast to the Southeast. These accounts make it perfectly clear that acts of prejudice and discrimination in America are not bounded by geographical borders, that they are common elements in the academic world, and that those who practice them often pay little or no heed to the intellectual accomplishments or the professional achievements of African Americans.

Though there is variation from one chapter to another in terms of style of presentation, length, and the degree of specificity provided by the author, each contribution offers a personal, sometimes painful, testimony of struggle and achievement, of challenge and success. Remember, however, that these accounts are from survivors—people who were strong enough and lucky enough to overcome the obstacles that were put before them. It is critical to acknowledge that there are other African Americans like them, perhaps equally as talented, who succumbed to the suffocation of racism in the system of higher education, and who thus have never been able to put their skills and abilities to the fullest use in predominantly white colleges and universities.

Motivation and Inspiration

The eminent African American sociologist W. E. B. DuBois speaks about the "twoness" that African Americans feel, the sense of duality in being at the same time a part of and apart from the American social order. DuBois's salient observations were made at a time when racial segregation was entrenched, either by law or custom, in much of the United States, and the effect was felt as strongly in colleges and universities as in other social institutions. In theory, this circumstance was changed by the civil rights struggle and the move toward desegregation that followed, but the reality is somewhat different. Institutions of higher education continued to follow traditional patterns of appointment, with predominantly white institutions selecting top administrators who were white, and usually male, while talented African American administrators found themselves restricted to the historically black colleges and universities. Michigan State University and later the State University of New York were notable exceptions to this rule as each of these institutions hired Clifton Wharton, an African American, first as president of the former institution, then later as chancellor of the latter.

Upon my entry into the academic community as a young professional in the early 1970s, I was fortunate to gain faculty and administrative experiences in settings as varied as a community college, an Ivy League university, and a private liberal arts college, and it was certainly striking to me that there was a noticeable absence of African Americans in high-level administrative positions in any of these institutions, or others with which I was familiar. By the late 1970s and early 1980s, I was working at a state-supported research university, and it was there that a series of events occurred that began to focus my interest on this topic. The Black Faculty and Staff Association at the university nominated a candidate for the provost's position at this institution when the new president initiated a search. The strongest candidate by far was an individual who was then serving as dean of the Graduate School of a Big 10 university, but there were two concerns about this person. One was that he shared the same disciplinary background as the president; the other was that he was African American, or in transparent coded terms, the candidate of the BFSA. To the credit of the search committee and the president, this individual was recommended, offered the position, and accepted it, thus becoming one of the very few such individuals to hold such an office. Even now, more than a decade and half later, only about a half-dozen African Americans have held positions of chief academic officer or chief executive officer of research I category universities.

The appointment of this individual to the provost's position led me to realize what the real impact of networking and sponsorship can mean. After he had gone through his period of transition, with his support, I competed in the campus review process to be the institutional nominee for the American Council on Education Fellowship Program in Academic Administration— arguably the higher education community's most selective and well known program for identifying and cultivating future administrative leaders. My application was selected to be forwarded by the campus to the ACE office for consideration, and I was later notified that I was chosen to be interviewed as a finalist for the program. Shortly before my interview, the provost arranged for me to meet a friend and colleague whom he was hosting for dinner. His guest was at that time the only African American chancellor of a Research I university in the country and has since added another distinction—that of becoming the first African American to be the CEO of both a public and a private predominantly white institutions of higher education. Having dinner and conversation with someone of this stature was an emotional high for me, and I gained some valuable insights as well as a connection that I have valued since that time.

Ultimately, I was awarded the fellowship, and the year of shadowing, meetings, campus visitations, and other professional activities with the other members of the cohort certainly expanded my understanding of the intricacies of the world of higher education and reinforced my perception that African Americans were underrepresented in both the faculty and administrative ranks, and my sense that this situation had less to do with the qualifications and availability of candidates than it did with the ethos of academe, which essentially reflects the values and practices of the larger society. Unlike several of my colleagues in the ACE program, upon completion of the fellowship, I chose to return to the faculty ranks rather than pursue an administrative position, partly because I wanted to explore the individual and institutional considerations that were at play in maintaining the often subtle, but still highly effective, practices of racism that are so clearly evident in colleges and universities.

As the editor of this volume, one feels a sense of collective pride in the accomplishments and achievements of the contributors, along with admiration at their abilities to work around or through personal and organizational roadblocks that were thrust into their paths. At the same time, these presentations elicit feelings of aggravation and bewilderment that this cadre of outstanding individuals had to endure the various challenges, taunts, epithets, and other forms of discourteous, offensive, and unprofessional behavior. At a time when a variety of misguided observations are being made from individuals as diverse in background as university regents to legislative officials to newspaper columnists that the playing field has been leveled for African Americans in higher education and elsewhere, these commentaries offer an insider's sense of what is really happening in the exalted world of academe. They tell us that skin color is still an important factor in terms of how people are treated as they carry out their responsibilities.

Tomorrow and Thereafter

African Americans who are currently making their way up the administrative ladder experience unpleasant encounters that are distressingly similar to the ones faced by their predecessors. These situations are likely to continue to occur until white academic leaders, administrators, and faculty signal to their colleagues and counterparts, in clear, specific language that racist behavior will not be tolerated and racist attitudes will not be countenanced. This message must come from those persons who are part of the majority and who have earned the confidence, respect, and admiration of their colleagues, because when it is articulated by African Americans, it is dismissed as defensive and paranoid. But when it comes from their friends and associates, their mentors and allies, their golf and bridge partners, then the message of inclusion and opportunity will begin to be considered in a different way than it has been in the past and is in the present.

The American dream has yet to be realized by many of its citizens. In the higher education arena, particularly within predominantly white colleges and universities, African Americans have systematically been denied the same opportunities to serve and lead that have been made available to other citizens. This legacy from the past does not have to continue into the future, and institutions of higher education can and should show the way for other social institutions to be more inclusive of African Americans in leadership positions. The contributors to this volume have sacrificed their privacy so that the indignities that they faced might be eliminated from the academic environment and to help all of us recognize the frightful truth that those who do not understand the past are doomed to repeat it.

Succeeding against the Odds in Higher Education: Advancing Society by Overcoming Obstacles Due to Race and Gender

REATHA CLARK KING

Introduction

Institutions of higher education are uniquely important for helping America achieve lasting progress in race relations in this country. Therefore, it is a delight for me to reflect on my experiences in higher education administration and to share my story with others who are interested in the adjustment of individuals in these institutions, in the contributions of the institutions to communities, and to the welfare of our country. In the aftermath of the major civil rights movement, a great deal already has been said about problems related to discrimination toward people because of race. Two thoughts persuaded me to offer my observations. One is that most of what has been shared with those of us who had the pioneer experiences fighting against racial segregation is not in written form so that others, especially younger professionals can refer to it. Second, the civil unrest of the past few years and the present tensions between the races indicate that individuals, organizations, and communities might benefit from some written information on how minorities coped as they helped to integrate situations in which different races had not worked together.

Events such as the Los Angeles riots, the focus on minorities in the presidential elections, and the many class action suits against organizations because of alleged discrimination against individuals all indicate that even with the gains of the civil rights movement, much more work needs to be done before our society is confident about its ability to deal with the diversity in its population. While I have focused on the values and attitudes of organizations and their impact on individuals, a complementary concern is about the possible benefits to the country from having us as a people learn not just how to live with diversity, but how to profit from diversity as well. How can we lower the tensions across racial differences, so people can relax, produce, and thus help increase the profitability or success of their organizations? So today there is much at stake in dealing successfully with issues of racial diversity. One benefit, and our main objective, is fairness to individuals. Another benefit is the increased productivity of organizations when their employees relax and work well together, and how this impacts the American economy.

The First Black Woman President: Developing a Frame of Mind to Succeed against Obstacles of Race and Gender

Becoming president of Metropolitan State University of Minnesota in 1977 was a unique experience for me, the Minnesota community, and the national higher education scene. At the time, this appointment carried a double challenge related to my race and to my gender, to be the first black woman president of a public university in Minnesota. This was just over twenty years ago, but it certainly was a different era, an unusual time in America, a time of social change for women and minorities. There were few women college and university presidents, and most of these were in religious and indepen- dent institutions. There were also far too few women in other leadership roles in higher education administration. Judging by people's reactions to my ap- pointment, it was clear that all across the country as well as in the state of Minnesota, many people desired change. They applauded my appointment, as shown by the numerous newspaper articles and editorials and welcoming letters. In the three weeks between my appointment in August 1977 by the Minnesota State University Board and my return to Minnesota with my fam- ily on Labor Day, I had received many encouraging letters from both strang- ers and friends in other states and in Minnesota.

In 1977, President Jimmy Carter of Georgia was inaugurated as president of the United States that year, and with him as vice-president was Walter "Fritz" Mondale of Minnesota. As I met people who had read and thought about my being a native Georgian moving with my family to Minnesota, they would laugh and say: "Here's another combination of grits and Fritz!" Hubert H. Humphrey, Sr., was still living, and his was a household name for our parents and relatives back in the South. Our families had long admired him because of the way he championed civil rights for all people. They identified with Hubert Humphrey and because of him, they had warm feelings about Minnesota.

However, even with these warm greetings upon my arrival, I came into the situation realizing that the combination of my being black and a woman in those days meant for me double the amount of glory if I succeeded and double the potential pitfalls that existed because of race and gender. There was strong public consciousness of my race and gender. To some, I was different because of my being a black president, and to others, I was different because I was a woman president. But fortunately for me, there were some with whom I became acquainted early in my presidency, who were not so preoccupied with either my race or my gender and who saw me as potentially a very effective president. This situation, coupled with the generally open Minnesota environment for government and addressing public issues, presented a real fishbowl for my work.

It became clear to me early on that I would have to extend myself and reach out to people, to help them become comfortable in working with me. The real issue was how to team with others who did not know me and who in many ways were different from me. As the institution's leader, it was soon very apparent to me that the position of president was truly different from all others in the university. Like the position at the top of any organization, mine was a special responsibility (or burden) to set a proper tone and shape the values and attitudes of the institution so that it was welcoming to all kinds of diversity, including the diversity of employees, along with my own special diversity. I did not have the luxury of thinking just about myself, but as leader of the organization I had to ensure that discriminatory practices did not exist toward others as well. There was no magic way for me personally to accomplish this desired outcome, except to draw on the many lessons I had learned from my prior family, schooling, and work experiences. This background was excellent preparation for facing both the deep joys and the disappointing experiences that I would have over the next eleven years.

Everything in race relations in our society in 1977 indicated to me that in order for me to succeed in higher education administration, I, as a black woman, would need to have an uncommonly strong commitment to social change and determination to succeed in the job. This frame of mind as I began my studies and employment in higher education administration had been shaped prior to my coming to Metropolitan State to serve as its president. Including my eleven years as president of Metropolitan State University, my work in predominantly white institutions had spanned thirty years. It began with my graduate studies in chemistry at the University of Chicago, which was followed by employment at the National Bureau of Standards as a research chemist, employment at York College of the City University of New York, and business studies at Columbia University just before I came to Metropolitan State. Because I had so few black colleagues, I felt very much like a "pioneer" in each of these situations—often feeling lonely and the disadvantage of cultural isolation, but feeling at the same time greatly fulfilled by the challenge of the work and the tremendous intellectual stimulation.

My sense of mission was unusual and actually focused on accomplishing two kinds of objectives. One objective was to further the purposes of the organizations, and my other objective was to help pave the way to opportunity for other blacks and women, as well as for myself. I was very conscious of this latter responsibility, so much so that I expected myself to be able to deal with bad treatment because of gender and race as it happened, and not to let it sidetrack me from my major objectives. With this frame of mind, it is possible that I, like many others in my generation, overlooked some offenses that we would react to very strongly today. The "first blacks" or "first women," or the first of any group that has a history of discrimination against it, carries a torch for others—those who sacrificed so we could be there, and those of us who will come later.

Like other young blacks in my generation, my unusual determination to persevere and try to succeed against the odds was strengthened constantly by my memory of relatives in earlier generations who were forbidden to even dream of such opportunities for themselves. We were always made aware that our experiences as "the first black" and "the first woman" were clearly were not undertaken for our benefit alone, but they were for the benefit of our whole race, and especially for those who did not have the earlier opportunity. We represented the pride of older blacks, and we were the inspiration for the younger blacks. We were expected to go away, do well, and then share our income with parents so they could take care of their basic needs and services that their low incomes could not cover. These expectations were indications that we had to succeed with whatever problem we encountered and that it would be a terrible disappointment to them if we failed to achieve our objective to get an education and better jobs than they had. It was quite clear that as the first blacks to have opportunity, we had to succeed if the numbers of us in the positions could ever increase. Similarly, as a black woman, a lot was riding on my success in order to open up more opportunities for women.

The Preparation Years: Conquering Poverty and Discrimination with Hard Work, Faith, and Early Visions of a Better Life!

My commitment to the elimination of racism and discrimination began to be shaped during my early years in segregated south Georgia, and since that time, this commitment has been honed and reinforced over and over by successes, joys, and disappointments.

The teachings from my family and community during my early upbringing in rural south Georgia have been a dominant influence on my life in later years. I learned some valuable lessons from my sharecropper family, my grandmother, and family friends in our impoverished community, and I have applied these lessons consistently in leadership positions in higher education administration and in my other jobs.

My immediate family consisted of five—my mother, father, two sisters, and myself. We sharecropped with white landowners. Our parents were highly respected by both whites and blacks for their work ethics and "the way they carried themselves." Both were from large families. My father, Willie, who never learned to read and write was one of thirteen children. My mother, Ola, who attended school to the third grade, was one of twelve children. Daddy's nickname was "Preacher" because of the way he prayed in church. So the respect my parents could not get because of formal education, they achieved in our community because of their personal qualities and the way they treated others. I was particularly impressed by how frequently our other relatives talked about how much everybody liked Preacher and Ola. The community generally respected those who were hard working, friendly to others, and sincere. My parents were great examples of these traits, and my sisters and I began early to imitate these behaviors.

Mainly for convenience to my mother, I began school at age four. As in other families, I was sent to the school with my older sister, Mamie, to be kept there while my mother worked in the field. Ours was a one-room school-house, Mt. Zion Baptist Church, which was the community's regular church, located outside of Pavo, Georgia. For our mostly illiterate rural community, "education" in those days was viewed both as a "tool" and as a "weapon"— a tool that we young people were encouraged to use to work our way out of the poverty, and a weapon that which individuals could use to overcome the oppressive forces of segregation that we black southerners knew well.

The role of our community members was to encourage us, and they certainly did a good job at that. Our teacher for all seven grades, Miss Florence Frazier, also lived in the neighborhood, and she talked about her students to the neighborhood people. She was a role model for everyone. Because of this close contact between the teacher and the community, word was spread to the community about which children were smart in school and made good grades. As word got around we would be encouraged by the whole neighborhood to use our good minds, study hard, get an education, so we could go away, get good jobs, and earn decent pay. Members of the community would say, "Get an education. Nobody can take that away from you." The saying that "it takes a whole village to educate a child" was certainly practiced there.

The community was very conscious of being robbed of what we had earned sharecropping for whites. Often at the end of the crop season, families would be told that they had borrowed all that was due them from the sale of the crops. Therefore, they had nothing coming to them for their work for the year. Their suspicion that they were constantly being cheated out of what was owed to them gave them strong reasons to encourage us children to work hard to become educated because no one could take that away from you. At very young ages, we could see that the community was depending on us "to make something out of ourselves."

For the most part the assumption in our south Georgia community was that blacks generally would have to leave the community in order to better themselves. Blacks who wanted a better life would leave and go up north to work as my mother did a few years later. Some of the men were later called to the armed services. While the community was mindful of the risks, they also cheered the economic benefits, the monthly pay that dependents would receive. By the early forties, there must have been talk about the work of the NAACP and integration in Georgia, but we did not hear about this in our communities. At that time it was risky for blacks to let whites know that they had thoughts about integration and social changes.

Fearing that they would be suspected of wanting to start trouble, blacks did not talk openly in the community about the need for social change. It was less risky to talk about the need for change in the homes and at church.

Our outside news came mostly through word of mouth from whites, from blacks who traveled, and from occasional copies of the *Pittsburgh Courier*, the black newspaper which would eventually get to our community. Even to this day, I can see the pink pages of the paper that would be lying around our house long after they were outdated. We would read in these papers over and over about outstanding blacks—morticians, doctors, presidents of the historically black colleges, and musicians—all of whom lived in other places. These were our black leaders and role models. We never saw them, but they were our symbols of success, examples of what we young people could go away and become if we applied ourselves in school.

World War II caused lots of shifting in our lives. My father did not go into the army but several of my mother's brothers did. Memories are still fresh in my mind of the rationing of gas and the arguments amongst relatives over who would have use of the coupons and get gas in their car. My grandfather had died, so my grandmother was alone and needed someone to live with her. I was drafted to live with my grandmother near Merrillville, Georgia, when I was in about the fourth grade. I transferred to attend school in nearby Coolidge, Georgia. During this time my mother and father separated and my father went to Belle Glade, Florida, to live with one of his sisters and to work as a migrant farm laborer. Later he worked in the sugar cane industry.

While I lived with my grandmother, three of her sons were serving in World War II. They assisted her financially. She eagerly looked forward to getting mail from them, and she also like to write back to them. Because she could not write, she would dictate the letters to me. At ten years old, I would write for her, and what a heady experience this was for me. I also taught her how to write her name. During these letter-writing sessions, she would explain to me how difficult it was for her to ask people to write for her. So whatever there was to master in school, I was able to do without difficulty and therefore could read and write for her with confidence.

Writing letters for my grandmother was the beginning of my preparation to be president of Metropolitan State University. Shaping an institution's mission and working like mad to help accomplish this mission is the real work of a college president. My illiterate grandmother and my father helped to prepare me. Watching them, I grew to understand well at an early age the kind of dignity people are deprived of when they do not have the opportunity to get an education, when they cannot read and write.

My grandmother, Mamie Watts, was a bold, friendly, and lively woman who loved church and who was quite a spirit in her community. She had given birth to thirteen children, and raised twelve of them. She had energy to spare and a strong sense of whether things were done properly. She would often say, "If anything is worth doing, it's worth doing right."

Going to church was our recreation as well as a great spiritual experience, and this filled most of our time. Because the church was across the road from our house, getting there was easy. Along with writing letters, our other activities included going to the store, going to school, visits by my mother and sisters, and occasionally going to work in people's fields. There was no car, so my grandmother and I walked everywhere unless someone gave us a ride. I have clear memories of the long, dusty road leading from our house and the many times we walked that road. The day the war ended grandmother and I met a white man on that road who said to her, "Mamie I have good news for you. The war is over!" She replied, "Thank God Almighty. My boys can come home!"

Then there was another transition. My mother, now a single parent, learned about better paying work up north. She decided to have my sisters live with my grandmother also while she went to New Jersey to work. She worked as a maid, which was similar to the kind of work that she sometimes did when we lived in Pavo, Georgia, but the pay was much better. She stayed away in New Jersey for about a year, living with Aunt Lessie, one of my grandmother's sisters. My mother was very attentive to us children, and she constantly sent money to my grandmother to help care for us.

Even though she had to be away from home to support us, my sisters and I were always aware that my mother cared deeply about us. We were her greatest concern. My mother returned from New Jersey when I was in the sixth grade and took me and my sisters to live with her. We lived in several small towns before we settled down in Moultrie, Georgia, where I attended high school. Generally, my sisters and I were good students and well disciplined, so our adjustment in the various schools was easy. Our transient lifestyle did not seen to affect our performance in school, and I would credit this to my mother's attentiveness. Somehow, we children had confidence in her; she represented stability for us.

Finally, we settled in Moultrie, Georgia, which I now call my hometown, Before we moved to Moultrie, my older sister had started in the high school, riding the school bus from the smaller town of Funston, Georgia, where we then lived. In a very excited tone, she would tell me about this more sophisticated setting with the older students and fancier teachers. My adjustment to the city high school a year later was easier because my older sister was already familiar with the teachers and many of the students. With a population then of 25,000 people, Moultrie was much larger that the small rural towns that we had lived in before that time.

We were studious and industrious and made a good adjustment to our new experiences in Moultrie. In little time, we were excelling both in the classroom and in the cotton fields. My mother stayed busy by combining housework and field work for different families. From time to time, she took my sisters and me to the field with her and taught us how to work. For certain families, she would let us go to the field without her while she would go to work in people's houses. Early on, my older sister Mamie and I acquired a reputation for being some of the best field workers around. Both of us excelled in picking cotton and stringing tobacco. On a given day, my sister and I and would pick more than two hundred pounds of cotton *each* when she was thirteen and I was twelve. We would get up early (around 4:00 A.M.) to get to the cotton field.

When my mother needed money badly enough, we would be kept out of school in the springtime to go to the field and chop cotton. There were a number of bad things about this situation. Both my sister and I loved school, and we really did not like to stay out of school at anytime to go work in the field. At the time, it was not uncommon for black children to be kept out of school to work in the field in the spring or to be late starting school in the fall because they were kept out to help finish gathering the cotton. This situation was particularly annoying because the white children of the farmers we helped were attending school while we were being kept out of school to work on *their* farms.

Only the heavens knew how much we disliked picking cotton as our main opportunity to earn money. The hot sun, heavy cotton sacks, gnats, dust, and dirt all made it terrible work for just three dollars per hundred pounds of cotton or six dollars per day if you could pick two hundred pounds each like we did. It was really hard work, and having to get up a 4:00 A.M. made it even worse. However, that assured us of earning more because we could pick the cotton while the morning dew was still on it and when it would weigh more. My sister Mamie and I both picked cotton until we left for college. We each declared that if we ever came back to a cotton field, we would own it. For both of us, the cotton fields were "fields of dreams," with our dreaming all the time we were there that this was short-term work for us because we were on our way to getting an education so we would have options for better work—work that paid more and that was less harsh.

We were diligent in pursuing work after school too. My mother remarried about midway through my high school years, and my stepfather worked in a mop and broom factory in Moultrie. That opened up an afterschool job at the factory where some days I worked two hours after school doing odd jobs such as painting broom handles. I also sometimes worked in people's homes after school. My sister and I learned to type and sew in school, and these skills served us well in getting along while in high school. On Saturdays we would sometimes go to the field and work until noon. On Saturday afternoon, we would sew and get our clothes ready for Sunday school and church activities the next day. In these church activities, my mother trusted us to the guidance of other women at the church—mainly Marie Jackson, Savannah Williams, and Miss Bridges. Mother rarely attended either these or our school events with us, feeling uncomfortable mainly because she had little education. At Mother Easter Baptist Church in Moultrie, Mamie and I were involved in the church choir, church clubs, and many of the special programs. Various other community people helped us with our extracurricular activities at church and school and would make sure that we had transportation home.

As we came closer to graduation from high school, we were quite focused on working to make ends meet for the family and planning for college expenses. Because Mamie and I were such good students, everyone in Moultrie assumed that we would go to college, even though they were well aware that my family could not pay our expenses. Mamie had always wanted to be a nurse, so she chose Dillard University in New Orleans and began at Dillard on a scholarship in September 1953. She chose Dillard because our high school principal had graduated from Dillard and knew about their outstanding baccalaureate program in nursing. Her experiences there were broadening for our whole family. When she returned for the Christmas holidays, she told us about that beautiful college campus in this far away city where the grass was green and all the buildings were white. She also talked about her college classmates from Texas who had so many clothes compared to hers, and her feelings about the difference between their families' means and ours. The fathers of several of her classmates were physicians. Her classmates had many material possessions that we could not afford.

Following in Mamie's footsteps, I graduated from high school and enrolled at Clark College in Atlanta in September 1954. Clark's dean of men was also the college recruiter, and he influenced me to attend Clark College. Mamie had helped me to prepare emotionally for leaving Moultrie to attend college in the big city of Atlanta. Both Clark College and Dillard University are historically black colleges and, similarly, both gave particular attention to the personal as well as the academic development of students such as Mamie and me, who came from small, segregated towns, and who were the first generation of our families to attend college. Highly motivated to do well as a means of overcoming the obstacles caused by segregation and discrimination against blacks, I began college at age sixteen at Clark College in Atlanta, Georgia, with a values orientation that has been continued in my later endeavors.

The Preparation Years (1954–58): Clark College—"Culture for Service, Second to None"

In September, 1954, I left Moultrie alone at age sixteen via Trailways bus to travel the two hundred miles to Clark College to begin my freshman year of college. My mother put me on the bus in Moultrie, with my trunk and other belongings, and I dutifully went to the back of the bus to the "colored" section. Prior to this trip, I had visited Atlanta once on a field trip with other students. Even though I had visited the campuses of Albany State College and Fort Valley State College while in high school, I had not visited the campuses of the black colleges in Atlanta. I knew Clark College from my conversations with its college recruiter who was also the dean of men, and from its literature showing pictures of its beautiful brick buildings. So this contact with the campus would be a totally new experience for me. The five-dollar one-way bus trip to Atlanta was about five hours, and this included several stops at other towns along the way, including Albany, Americus, and Griffin. (Usually in Americus, to and from Atlanta, I would get off the bus and use the toilet for "coloreds." Looking back on the experience, this was eventful because of the segregated facilities—some marked clearly for "colored" and others for "whites." This is another indication of how segregation was clearly an impediment to the progress of the nation, as well as to individual progress. It was an inefficient system and a tremendous drain on public and private resources. Think about the additional cost to an economy of maintaining two sets of toilets—one set for whites and one for blacks and the distraction of people's time to monitor whether "coloreds" were obedient and using the system.)

To get to Clark's campus, I took a cab from the bus station to my assigned dormitory, Merner Hall. Soon I met Phoebe Birney, the dean of women, and eventually assembled with other freshman women to be informed about the rules. Dean Birney was quite a striking woman, who modeled the style and behavior she wanted the young women to imitate. She was quite emphatic about three of the rules. The young women must be in the dorm by 6:00 P.M. and could sign out to the library from 6:00 to 9:00 P.M. We could not wear slacks on the campus—they were allowed only in the dorms— and we could not go barelegged on campus; we were required to wear socks or stockings all of the time on campus. I was assigned to Merner Hall with a roommate from Brunswick, Georgia, whose name coincidentally was also Retha. She was Retha Mae Davis, and I was Reatha Belle Clark.

My early adjustment was helped also by my need to report to my job in the registrar's office soon after arriving on campus. The job put me in touch with another network of friends, and I began a work routine that I would continue for four years at Clark—twelve hours per week for thirty-five cents per hour. I enjoyed that work, eventually moving up to be the transcript clerk in charge of mailing out transcripts upon the many requests from graduates and former students. Dean Birney, our house mothers in the dorms, and our work supervisors knew a lot about our backgrounds and started immediately to nurture our development so we could make a smooth transition into the more sophisticated environment which we had not known back at home. It took me a while to get rid of the sun burn and remnant dirt in my skin from the cotton patch and the stain on my hands and body from gathering tobacco. But I finally did get cleaned up and happily worked into the wonderful new routine of my college life. For me, Clark College provided a superb blend of cultural and academic education. These experiences at Clark were a critical link in the chain of activities that prepared me for successful work in predominantly white universities.

Along with the fine academic program, Clark College helped me to see clearly why knowledge of one's culture is so helpful for getting along and how this can contribute to one's quality of life. Even though the Supreme Court had handed down its school desegregation ruling in 1954, the year I entered Clark College, the message to blacks from the broader community continued to be a message of degradation, saying in so many ways that we were inferior people and that we were unworthy of respectful treatment. There was great concern in my hometown of Moultrie, Georgia, over how the court's desegregation decision would be implemented. My college education effectively counteracted these negative messages with which blacks were indoctrinated by the broader community.

Influenced by the powerful college motto Culture for Service, Second to None, I received in my education at Clark a handle on both my own culture and the academics; I became introduced to new kinds of work for young women. In many ways, Clark communicated to its students that we were not inferior people, but that we were beautiful people, and that we were capable of making contributions in the various kinds of jobs. At Clark, the studies were challenging, the people were truly impressive, and the music was terrific. Chapel attendance was required, and we had a special program at each session. Often we had guest speakers who were also great role models.

However, even with such good experiences, it was not an absolutely perfect world for me at Clark. Two problems plagued me throughout my four years of college. One was financial need and the other was career aspiration. Even with a scholarship and a very regular job in the registrar's office, I still had difficulty paying my bills and would have to see the president of the college each semester to get special permission to take my final examinations because my bill was not paid. This was humiliating and very stressful. I so much envied other students who did not have financial worries.

In the meantime, my sister Mamie was progressing well in her nursing studies at Dillard University and also performing mightily as family leader to counsel us through severe financial hardships—helping me meet ends at Clark and helping my mother through some health problems. When my mother needed surgery, the question was how would she pay for it? Alongside this situation was a decision to be made whether I would yield to friends' invitation to run for election as "Miss Clark College" and to reign as the college queen during my senior year. This was quite an honor, but the wisdom of doing this really was a big issue because of the extra expense involved for my clothes. My sister encouraged me to do it, indicating that she would help purchase my clothes. She also encouraged mother to have the surgery she so desperately needed. Mamie had a plan for covering these expenses—she would join the army! During her junior year at Dillard University, she enrolled in the Army Nurses Corps primarily to help our family.

In choosing a career, there was the gender bias to deal with, a real problem that many women accepted as they resorted to careers that society deemed appropriate for them, rather than choosing for themselves. Women in those days were expected to choose teaching, nursing, or other careers that would be nonthreatening to men and compatible with the role of housekeeping. I arrived at Clark intent on becoming a home economics teacher. However, because of my fascination with freshman chemistry, which was required for a home economics major, I changed my mind during the first semester of my freshman year and decided to study to become a research chemist. Dr. Alfred S. Spriggs, chair of the chemistry department was very instrumental in this decision. He simply told me what a research chemist did and the education required, and he reassured me and other women students that we could do this very well. During Black History Month back at my high school in Moultrie, I had heard much about George Washington Carver, the famed scientist at Tuskegee Institute.

Women were expected to find a husband and not pursue more education. People, even some of my own relatives, would challenge this decision on my part because, in their opinion, no man would want a woman who attended graduate school and obtained more education than he had! This kind of advice was discouraging for many women. However, I simply ignored it. The excitement of chemistry and mathematics courses confirmed my interest in these fields of study and caused me to challenge the stereotypic notion about what were appropriate careers for women.

I also helped my financial situation at Clark by traveling north during the summer months and working as a live-in maid. Influenced by Dean Birney, I worked each of my college summers, beginning at age seventeen, as a maid in upstate New York. The long train ride to Pawling, New York, was an adventure for me. Similar to the way my mother had done while I was growing up, I too was now going north to find better work. There was one significant difference; I was earning to help pay my college expenses; she had been earning to help care for her young children whom she had left with her mother. After a brief visit to my family in Moultrie, Georgia, I would return to Atlanta and board the train for Pennsylvania Station in New York City, be met there by my host family, and then be driven to Quaker Hill near Pawling, New York, where I would work until the last week in August.

While living with these well-to-do white families, I had an unusual view from the inside, so to speak, and undoubtedly this influenced my style as later I was to reach out and get to know many people in my various careers. From talking with them and regular siteseeing in New York City, I learned a lot about the Northeast and what it was like to be "up north." They encouraged me in my efforts to get an education and helped me to learn. They showed a great interest in my family and in Clark College and were inquisitive about life for me in the South, which at the time was not integrated. Although I earned just twenty-five dollars per week at the time (and saved every penny of it!), this was my alternative to field work back at home, which would have been picking cotton and stringing tobacco again. So I opted for the maid job in New York and went there each of four summers after college, even during the summer between college and graduate school in 1958. Traveling to such unusual places at such a young age helped to condition me for the extensive foreign travels and speaking engagements that I have undertaken in later years. These kinds of experiences reinforced in me the belief that all experiences, big and little, can be useful in helping us learn how to deal with diverse situations in our future.

My four years at Clark College were more eventful than I ever imagined they would be when I entered as a freshmen. As class valedictorian, I graduated in May 1958 and, on a Woodrow Wilson Fellowship, enrolled in the University of Chicago in the fall of 1958 to begin graduate study in chemistry. I learned about the University of Chicago from several of my black college teachers who were graduates from that college. They and others spoke of the university's superb reputation for excellence. At twenty, I was formally launching my studies in predominantly white institutions where I would help pioneer and increase opportunities for more blacks for the next thirty years.

The University of Chicago (1958–62): A Unique Opportunity for Scholarship and Intellectual Growth

The University of Chicago was a truly exciting but very different experience from those I had known before. The experience was intellectually stimulating and intense from the first day, and remained that way throughout my stay at the university, which lasted for the four years and one quarter without interruption. Following my graduation from Clark in May, I worked as a live-in maid for three months in Pawling, New York, and then began my studies at the University of Chicago in September. After checking into Beecher Hall, one of the dormitories for graduate women students, I was introduced to the resident hall assistant, met some of my dorm mates, and then found the chemistry department and introduced myself to some of the administrators. Particularly warm and friendly was Dr. Parsons in the chemistry department. He seemed to have the answer to every question that came up.

Soon I met Professor Clements, my faculty advisor, and held my first meeting with him to get my assigned courses for the first quarter. We compared the textbooks that we had used at Clark with the kinds of textbooks the professors at Chicago would suggest. Also in this meeting, Professor Clements gave me some direct advice, specifically warning me that the course would be challenging because the faculty would go faster than probably I was accustomed to at Clark, and he thought the textbooks would be more challenging. Finally, he alerted me to the difference in the students—specifically that my classes at Chicago would consist of the top students from a large variety of schools. At Clark, I had been one of the best students compared to the rest.

As Professor Clements had warned, the classes for first-year graduate students were larger, the assignments were heavy, and I noticed immediately a difference of which he had not warned me. There were very, very few blacks and women in the classes. This was not surprising to us in 1958, as there were mostly white males in the advanced levels of the physical sciences in 1958, and the scarcity of minorities and women would get a little worse as I moved into the advanced levels of my studies in chemistry at the university. I became good friends with the few women and blacks there. I constantly checked on their progress, and they did likewise with me.

I completed the coursework and chose physical chemistry. I passed the preliminary examination for the doctorate degree and began research for my dissertation under the mentorship of professor Ole Kleppa. Kleppa was a member of the chemistry department and the Institute for the Study of Metals. The chemistry department had two main social events for students, faculties, and their families. These events were the annual holiday party during the Christmas season and a summer picnic, and I participated in both.

During my stay at the university, I was deeply involved in my studies, scholarship, and intellectual pursuits most of the time. This seemed to be the case with other students and faculty to the point that there was not as much consciousness about racial differences as one would expect. In the dormitory, there were people studying social work, history, and English, and they also were deeply involved in their studies. Budgeting to make ends meet, keeping up with the challenging studies, and keeping warm in the Chicago winter were some of our preoccupations. We sometimes commented among ourselves that the campus was not the real world. The civil rights movement and its impact throughout the country, the 1960 Democratic National Convention and the nomination of John F. Kennedy for president, and the visits to Rockefeller chapel by giants such as Benjamin F. Mays and Martin Luther King, Jr., inspired me persist in my efforts to succeed at Chicago.

Compared to my four years at Clark, my financial worries had become considerably relieved at the University of Chicago. The Woodrow Wilson Fellowship helped to get me started, and when it expired, the university provided me additional fellowship and research assistantships. By then my sister was becoming well established in her career in the Army Nurse Corps and was able to provide some financial support to my mother and younger sister, who by then had graduated from high school and enrolled in Fisk University in Nashville, Tennessee. During my first two years at Chicago, the State of Georgia provided tuition assistance, which it did under a strange provision of assisting black students who had to go out of state for graduate work that they could not obtain at a black public institution in the State of Georgia. My sister Mamie had obtained assistance from the State of Georgia for her nursing studies at Dillard University. Following her advice, I completed the application form for assistance and mailed it to the appropriate state office in Georgia. Before long, I was called to the university's business office and informed that they were holding a check for me from my home state! This support stopped when the white universities in Georgia became integrated. This incident shows another way in which segregation was costly to states. Although financial assistance was helpful to me, it facilitated the brain drain from the state, because the state itself was essentially exporting its talented people. My sister and I laughed about it, but there is really nothing funny about discriminating against people and then trying to patch up a response to the problem.

To give myself a break and to earn some additional funds, I decided to take off a summer and work in Washington, D.C., where my older sister lived. To help her with living expenses while I was there, I set out looking for a summer job. Jobs were not generally open for blacks at that time. This situation was confirmed when I answered a newspaper ad by an agency that said it had lots of domestic jobs open at an embassy. After calling and being told the same, I went to the agency to complete the necessary application form. I entered and requested the form, but the minute the gentleman saw my face, he said that all the jobs had been filled. It was clear to me that blacks were not welcomed. Soon afterward, I took the civil service test for clerical employment, scored very high, and became a clerk typist at the General Accounting Office. Essentially, the job involved typing reports on claims by federal employees who had been injured on the job. It seemed that every form on my desk involved a dog bite to a mail carrier, so I left there after three months, realizing for sure that carrying mail can be a hazardous occupation. As I returned to school and completed my studies at the University of

Chicago, I soon learned firsthand that getting a job in my field would be tricky because of my race and gender. It was never clear to me which would be the bigger barrier, but both were factors.

Many interviewers came to the campus, but they had definite concerns about professional women job seekers. The interviewers' big concern was whether a woman would get married. The next issue was, if you got married, whether you would have children. The interviewers seemed to be uneasy about interviewing both minorities and women. Eventually, my dissertation advisor informed me that in Washington, the Naval Research Laboratory and the National Bureau of Standards had vacancies that I might apply for. I was offered positions by both and accepted a position in the Heat Division of the National Bureau of Standards.

I completed my studies for the Ph.D. degree at Chicago at the end of the fall quarter in 1962, left to begin employment at the National Bureau of Standards in Washington, and then returned for the commencement ceremony on a beautiful day in April 1963. This was shortly after I reached age twenty-five. By then I had married, and my husband, Judge, was studying for his Ph.D. in chemistry at Howard University in Washington, DC.

The National Bureau of Standards (1963-68): Experiencing the Power of Scientific Research

The National Bureau of Standards (NBS) is a unique organization, and it was a most impressive place to work for young scientists in 1963. It employed some of the best scientists in the country and had an international reputation for the quality and precision of its measurements. Among our people in the Heat Division were some of the country's best known basic and applied scientists in their fields. The scientists seemed confident. My job showed me that scientists are powerful people because of their knowledge and the influence of their work on all the rest of society. For young, developing minds, the atmosphere was very stimulating. My confidence grew from my employment and productivity at NBS.

However, the possible limitations that existed because of race and gender were very clear, and there were issues to deal with because of both of those things. Soon after arriving, I learned from colleagues that I had been selected for employment because my supervisor, George Armstrong, was especially interested in hiring a black and was sure *not* to overlook a qualified black candidate who appeared on the civil service list. I learned later that George Armstrong was clearly interested in social change and wanted to begin taking the initiative to help end discrimination in the employment of blacks. He seemed delighted when I expressed interest in employment at NBS, and he welcomed me to his group, the rest of which was white and male except for the secretary who was a white woman.

This situation underscores how change tends to happen when predominantly white institutions take the initiative and attract and involve more minorities. Quite often there is a committed individual who is willing to stick his or her neck out, step forward, and *act,* setting the example and starting the change.

George Armstrong's style taught me a lot about how to get things done when I later moved into supervisory positions at York College and at Metropolitan State University. It is best to spend more time doing something than talking about doing it.

George Armstrong was a quiet person, a good mentor and supervisor, and from the beginning, he encouraged me to extend myself and approach all other units of the NBS for help as I needed it. He assigned me some tough projects to direct. After two brief orientation studies in our laboratory, I was given responsibility for a special project supported by the Advanced Research Projects Agency (ARPA) to determine the heat of formation of oxygen difluoride. This project also involved measuring the heats of formation of some interhalogen compounds and many reactions between these compounds and the element hydrogen. The work was challenging because it required the original designs of flow calorimetric equipment that would resist corrosion by these materials, applications of computers, and the learning of new computer languages. I used every bit of material science that I had learned at the University of Chicago and more! I traveled and presented research papers at professional meetings.

During my employment at NBS, our two children were born, and what a thrill this was for our families. However, for me privately, there were some definite anxieties. Out of the 120 people in the division, there was only one other professional woman, Anna, and her husband was also a scientist at NBS. Anna was having children too, and she and I talked a lot about what people thought. The gender issue was very tricky to deal with because we knew many people, both men and women, frowned on our decision to work outside of the home. I dealt with this problem mainly by ignoring it.

As my family grew, I grew professionally, completing many excellent studies, several research publications, job promotions, and divisional recognition for the quality of our work in the project. Motivated by the need to carry on the dreams of both President John F. Kennedy and Dr. Martin Luther King, Jr., I left NBS in fall 1968 and moved to New York with my husband and two children, so my husband could accept employment as chair of the chemistry department at Nassau Community College in Garden City, New York. Both President Kennedy and Dr. King were assassinated while I worked at NBS. These were the low points of those nearly six years at NBS. But my good experiences there and these two events challenged me to continue carving out the path to opportunities for others.

Higher Education Administration (1968–77): York College and Achieving Respect for Being More Than an Affirmative Action Statistic

Thirty years old at the time, moving to New York with my husband and our two sons, ages 6 months and three and one-half years old, and well grounded professionally from my previous years at the National Bureau of Standards, I felt fully ready to plunge into a busy routine of being wife, mother, college teacher, and social activist—all New York style! And it all began with an intensity that I could not have imagined in my orderly, very highly professional environment at the National Bureau of Standards.

Reflecting the values and frustrations of a predominantly white college, York College for me was a blend of glory and pain that everyone should learn how to handle. You either thrive in such a situation, or you are killed by the hurt from charges that "You are just an old Uncle Tom!" as I was sometimes called by white liberals and their black sympathizers. The pressures in predominantly white institutions can readily polarize rather than cause unity among blacks. When you are a new kid on the block and come from a former work environment like NBS, how do you handle a situation that your colleagues, especially the nonscientists, do not understand? This was the case at York because so many of my colleagues there had come over from a sister CUNY institution when York opened. How do you handle activists' suspicions when they are unsure about whether you are in agreement with them or with "the establishment" on different issues that arise on campus? For me personally, the early situation at York College highlighted another peculiar situation that strained the environment as institutions were being integrated in the late sixties, and that is whether minorities were truly valued for their contributions to the institution or whether they were mere tokens and welcomed to the institutions because they counted as affirmative action statistics.

My nine years of employment at York College of the City University of New York began in 1968, which was just one year after the college opened. This was a period of strong activism and social change throughout American society. With all of the country struggling to carry out the written and unwritten mandates of the civil rights movement, this college and other predominantly white higher education institutions at the time were strongly affected by issues of access to educational opportunity, urban change, affirmative action, and the campus protests about the Vietnam War. Often at the faculty meetings, there were angry people filled with frustration about external decisions that affected them and the institutions and which they could not control.

Having operated just one year, York College had very little history of its own when I arrived in 1968. The history that most of its faculty knew was what they brought from their former institutions, which for the most part were the older sister CUNY colleges, especially Brooklyn College. Because they were so much in the majority, these faculty mostly shaped York's early values and attitudes about the employment of minority faculty and staff and the climate that so clearly affected our progress. Many of the senior administrative and faculty positions were already filled by faculty transferring from other institutions in the system, and this added to racial sensitivities about the attitudes that controlled the establishment of the campus. Even with the threat of continuing the practices at other CUNY institutions, a lot of things had to be developed for York from scratch, including the campus, curriculum, and various student services. The college's culture was strongly influenced by its temporary, or makeshift facilities and within two years these were quite spread out between the areas of Jamaica and Bayside, in the borough of Queens in New York City.

Although its facilities were temporary, the campus tensions at York College were very strong in its first two years, and these centered first on the issue of where the permanent campus would be situated—on a golf course in Fort Totten, which the president and most other whites favored, or as part of an urban renewal project in inner city Jamaica, Queens. This became very much a racial issue that sharply polarized York's faculty. The debate was partly fueled by the fact that the surrounding community in Jamaica was largely minority and the communities near Fort Totten were predominantly white. Along with several of my York colleagues, I worked tirelessly for the location of the college in Jamaica, and our position was favored in the final outcome. The decision to locate the campus in Jamaica, Queens, was eventually made by others outside of the campus, including the CUNY Board and city officials in the administration of Mayor John Lindsay. However, for several years the dispute continued among campus and community people about whether the decision was wise.

As if these challenges were not enough, the college was also dealing with the systemwide issues of open enrollment which had just been instituted throughout the City University of New York. Another big question being debated by the CUNY system was whether it was appropriate for the system to continue free tuition for students. At the same time as York College was settling its site decision and dealing with the systemwide issues, the campus became polarized among students and faculty over the Vietnam War.

All of the above situations provided a fertile setting for those of us who were confident of our skills and committed to positive societal change to help develop the institution and put in place some needed educational opportunities for students. This was a particularly exciting time for the college, for me, and for my family. It was a time for healing amongst colleagues who had so deeply offended each other in the heated faculty debates. As many of us plunged in to do all the work needed to establish this new college, there were many opportunities for me to work with fellow blacks and liberal whites who earlier had caused me the worst pain as they charged me with being an Uncle Tom.

The York College experience taught me that in responding to challenges, one must have a vision. Mine was a vision for positive social change, pursued through an interest in providing educational opportunity for others that is stronger than anyone can imagine. I learned at York that these beliefs and one's efforts to achieve them can be used to rally people of all races to work together—whether they are fellow minorities who are suspicious of you or whites who might question your competence to be in the institution.

For young, capable, and eager faculty and staff, there was much to be done and lots of opportunity to further one's development by helping out. Hired as an assistant professor of chemistry in 1968, I plunged right into this environment and worked hard at the college, at home, and in the community. My early work focused on a carefully planned routine, including caring for our young children, classroom teaching, and campus committee work. Over the nine years I advanced through the ranks of assistant and associate to full professor of chemistry and to the administrative posts of associate dean for natural sciences and mathematics and associate dean of faculty. I supervised undergraduate research students, succeeded in getting a research grant from the National Science Foundation, and performed extensive community service. Within the college, we shepherded facilities planning and construction of the new science building, development of some excellent new programs, and the hiring of outstanding faculty. Both our faculty and students in the sciences and mathematics disciplines were among the strongest in the college. Along with this full work schedule for me, we had a full family life at home. At home, everything for me was easier because our children were healthy and because we had reliable and quality day care services for them at the home of a community friend. They were not relatives, but our children knew them fondly as "Aunt Martha" and "Uncle David."

Some thirty years later, the institution today has a beautiful modern campus, is the centerpiece of the Jamaica community, and is a tremendous educational opportunity for younger and older students. It was well worth the struggles to help bring it into being.

Columbia University: Preparing for the Ultimate Responsibility

Assuming in those days that it would be difficult for a woman to advance in higher education administration, I chose to take a sabbatical leave while at York College, and after weighing some options very carefully, I decided to enroll in the business school at Columbia University in 1977. I was seeking additional academic knowledge for the financial management of organizations. Tremendously inspired by my work at York College and how this kind of education I would receive at Columbia could improve the quality of management in public sector jobs, I enrolled in Columbia fulltime as an older student, somewhat oblivious to the fact that I was different from most of the students and faculty, either because of my race, age, being married with children, science background, or because of the distance I commuted from Long Island. With a fine fellowship provided me by the Rockefeller Foundation, my thoughts were focused on becoming rejuvenated through new knowledge and relating this to the practical education I had received through work. Having taken advantages of all prior opportunities to learn helped tremendously with my adjustment to Columbia.

Additional preparation for the tasks at hand and reaching out to others are the key ways I have coped and worked well in predominantly white institutions. Surely there have been disappointments. I have "managed" them. These disappointments will depress, and possibly destroy one emotionally, if one does not manage them.

As unfair as it might be for minorities to have to do it, constant extra preparation economically, socially, and academically are helpful to our ability to adjust in situations where we are the minority. The more secure we feel with these attributes, the less conscious we are of the differences between ourselves and the environment and the less we care about how self-conscious others are about our presence. Equipped with these attributes we minorities are better able to relax and to perform like heck!

Business Policy, a capstone course in the twenty-course program at the Columbia business school was my transition experience to Metropolitan State. The course gave me the perspective of a chief executive officer of an organization, a feel for what it is like to be accountable for everything. When invited to apply for the presidency at Metropolitan State University, it was clear to me that I was ready for the position.

Metropolitan State University (1977–88): The University Presidency— Being Accountable for Everything

Metropolitan State University was six years old when I was appointed its president in August 1977. A young, nontraditional, baccalaureate-level institution for older students, the university was poised for exciting growth and development. Was it ready for a black woman president? Was the public ready for a black woman president? The great progress by the institution under my presidency would lead to the "yes" answer to this question. However, there were some painful experiences along the way that would cause me not to be able to give an unqualified "yes" in answering these questions.

Judging by its expansion in students, graduates, programs, fundraising, faculty and public appeal, and increased prestige, Metropolitan State was a tremendous success under my presidency. Between 1977 and 1988 the enrollment grew from 1,600 to 6,000 students and the number of graduates increased from 1,200 to 6,000. Along with improvements in the nationally recognized individualized degree program in the arts and sciences, a new baccalaureate degree program in nursing was added and new programs in computer science and accounting were planned. The institution added its first graduate program in management and administration. Support services to better serve women and minority students were established. Alumni relations, legislative relations, and public relations were strengthened. The Metropolitan State University Foundation was developed into a major support organization with outstanding and loyal trustees from the community and extensive fundraising to support the university. All through the years of my presidency, the graduates and students testified far and wide about the unique educational opportunity that Metropolitan State represented to them. The work of championing its mission to be a flexible and high-quality option for the working adults was a joy for me as president of the university.

Even with this success, the environment's readiness for a black woman president was tested. Three of my most difficult experiences in this regard are described here; two occurred without warning, and there was clear warning of the third.

The symbol of the first one showed in the opinion polls, common in the late seventies and early eighties, that questioned people of their thoughts about women versus men supervisors. The main message to women managers was clear: most employees preferred a male supervisor and some actually resented and resisted reporting to women. Some people were blatant and said openly, "I don't want no woman boss!"

Sometimes as president, one makes bad appointments and then suffers the consequences. This was my case as we appointed our first assistant to the president at Metropolitan State. Even though it was a part-time position, this was a real achievement in what turned out to be a very lean budget for an institution of our size. Once hired and positioned in a neat office, the individual appointed and I had started working together. Then came the day when I had some very critical items to work on related to our budget presentation to the state legislature, I asked my assistant to help with something, and she replied: "You do it yourself." This was a jolt. The immediate challenge to me was not to lose focus and to be able to delegate the disposition of this problem, rather than to become involved in a some kind of confrontation myself. Being able to delegate the disposition of problems is an advantage of the position of president. If hiring is done carefully, usually there are a number of persons a president can call on for help when one has special needs.

Fortunately for me, Metropolitan State University had one of the best directors of personnel in the world, Jan Anderson. Without missing a beat, I called Jan and requested that she take care of this situation. Jan followed up immediately. Absolutely confident that she would handle this situation in the best way, I went on to my committee hearing at the Minnesota State Capitol building. Jan always had ready some good alternative ways to solve problems, she was confident about taking charge and executing the best plan of action, and she could act quickly. Needless to say, the employee was not there when I returned from the State Capitol and I have not seen her since. After the incident, Jan and I never devoted a lot of time discussing whether the resentment was traceable to my race or gender. Some earlier discussions with the employee about a problematic divorce case she was involved in led me to think that it was resentment because of gender. However, one's imagination can run wild in situations like this, and perhaps mine was no different from others because this was an unusual incident. The key lesson to me from this incident was that in hiring another assistant, I had to tactfully search for the candidate who would be comfortable reporting to and working with a black female president. This need was important for me to consider in choosing my senior officers of the university as well. First of all, the individuals needed to be highly competent, but I also realized that any feeling of uneasiness toward me because of race and gender would hamper our overall productivity and thus had to be considered by me before the appointments were made.

Outside of the university there were similar jolts. The lessons for me were real and have been practiced ever since. The most disturbing occurred on August 1984, during our monthly meeting of the seven presidents of the state universities with the chancellor of the State University System. Routinely, we held this monthly meeting to discuss a range of issues pertaining to the welfare of the state universities, including governance, budget, personnel, legal, academic, and student services; and legislative relations. At this particular meeting, we were reviewing the items that would probably be submitted to the state legislature in the system's biennial budget request. I very much wanted my colleagues to agree to including a request for funds for Metropolitan State University to establish its Minority Services Program. Being urban and especially committed to improving access for underserved populations, the Metropolitan State University had set as a special goal to recruit more minority and women students and to improving the support services that would enable them to succeed. We had rallied the Metropolitan State University Foundation and friends in the community to support this special initiative.

At this meeting, my objective was to get my fellow presidents and the chancellor and his staff on board to support the request for funds from the legislature for this purpose. The amount asked for was less than $100,000, rather small in comparison to the total budget, but significant compared to our institution's budget. This meeting was on a Wednesday, just after the Democratic Convention had been held in San Francisco when Reverend Jesse Jackson and Governor Mario Cuomo gave their rousing speeches about the need for attention to domestic issues. I came to this particular president's meeting feeling a special sense of urgency to take stronger action to improve services to minority students. Jon Wefald, who later became president of Kansas State University, was chancellor of the Minnesota State University System, and he was presiding at our meeting. As I argued for including this item in the system's budget request to the legislature, it became clearer and clearer that my colleague, the other presidents were either unenthusiastic or not moved enough to speak in support of my request. They responded as though this item did not belong in the overall budget request. The hurt I felt at that moment led to a very strong response from me which caused the chancellor immediately to adjourn the meeting for a break. After the break, the chancellor mentioned to me on the side, "We are going to find some funds for this program."

I left this meeting relieved by the chancellor's interest but disappointed by the response of my colleagues. I neither brought the item back to a system presidents' meeting; nor did I go around the chancellor and fellow presidents to discuss it with individual legislators, nor did I discuss it with members of the State University Board. I appealed to the Metropolitan State University Foundation to press forward to help find private resources to establish the services, and it did. This became one of the finest services of its kind on any campus in Minnesota.

Years later, the Minnesota State University System instituted a major program in cultural diversity. However, it was done on the timeline desired by the majority. My request, though extremely important to me as a black president, was ahead of its time, and I could not understand why others could not share my sense of urgency, which perhaps was similar to Martin Luther King, Jr.'s when he explained to the Birmingham clergy why he could not "wait" with the goals of the civil rights movement. The word *wait* is particularly frustrating to women and minorities when they are trying to help institutions act and implement changes to overcome problems related to past injustices to women and minorities. In moments such as these, women and minorities are easily caused to feel that they are of "marginal" value to the organization. This experience highlights a situation that frequently happens as minorities bring forth proposals and suggestions for change in predominantly white institutions. By the time there is courage to voice the proposal, the proposer usually feels a strong sense of urgency for taking action. A suggestion by the majority to wait or delay taking action has to be accompanied by extraordinarily good reasons in order to minimize frustration in the proposer.

When changes in the higher education institutions are needed, on whose timeline will changes be implemented—on one that responds to the sense of urgency that minorities feel, or on a timeline that is deemed appropriate by the majority? Ideally, these two timelines will be the same, but quite often they are not.

Organizations can reduce racial tensions if they choose to move with a sense of urgency in making their environments hospitable to minorities, rather than delay by choosing a longer timeline. Many suggestions that minorities make do not cost money, and it would help if the persons in charge of approving would just say, "Go ahead and do it."

A third situation points out what happens when we are trying to remedy problems by going up against a power structure. Seeking to gain approval for my institution to offer new degree programs presented particular challenges because Metropolitan State University was a new institution. In our system, many levels had to approve, but the Higher Education Coordinating Board worried us most. Somehow, in our minds we worried that they either favored or were concerned about whether the larger local institutions would object, and we were mostly concerned about the University of Minnesota and the then College of St. Thomas. On April 1985, we were concluding a very long review process and seeking final approval to offer the university's first master's degree program in management and administration. My concern was that the politics rather than the substance and the need would be pervasive in the Coordinating Board's decision.

The vice chancellor of academic affairs had alerted me that the vote would be very close and probably the proposal would be defeated. Facing an all white board and the stress of the moment, surely I was mindful of my race, my gender, the youth of my university, and the lack of "clout" compared to that the larger institutions were perceived to have. Yet I was absolutely determined that the program was right because our students and the public needed the option. If the other universities were so great, why were they not serving this clientele? With a feeling of absolute confidence that the students who would enter this program deserved to be served, I stood before the board and answered their questions with confidence, and the program was approved. Some of the questions were hostile, and they helped my determination. Both Peter McGrath, then president of the University of Minnesota, and Mary Thornton Phillips, chancellor of the Minnesota Area Technical Institutes offered compelling and supportive comments.

This hearing was in a crowded room, but it was a lonely experience for me. I went in, feeling emotionally armed for a struggle and expecting outright bigotry because of my awareness of the concerns of some of the board members. More than the power imbalance, the key question was what was really at stake here? It was program opportunities for students. My courage and confidence were clearly bolstered by an unshakable belief that people's work opportunities would be increased by this program and that the public needed and deserved this option. Those who held power and who controlled what institutions could do needed to prove to me that this program should and could not be offered to the public, as much as I needed to prove to them that my institution should be permitted to offer it. At times like this, it was most important for me to focus on eliminating injustice for people that is caused by neglect.

My championing the needs of the public did not protect me from receiving hate mail and public threats with which I also had to learn how to deal during my presidency. There were times when I experienced considerable private anguish because of public threats directed to me to or other black people. Some of these situations were particularly frightening and caused me at times to be concerned for our children. One was a letter from a mixed up person, or possibly it was just a mixed up letter from a person who would otherwise be considered normal. Obviously this person thought my husband was white. It went on and on with statements to the effect that "GOD don't like these mulatto children. He did not intend for the races to mix. The Bible did not intend for the races to marry each other." When my secretary handed me the letter, she apologized and said, "I just hated to give you this letter, but I felt that I should."

Another incident involved a call to the principal of my children's school inquiring about what we had planned to do after school. The caller warned that we had better watch out. The third was a call to my Minnesota State University Board office inquiring about where the president of Metropolitan State University would be that weekend, and a comment that I had better watch out. The chancellor's assistant called to inform me about this call, and then she apologized. It is not unusual for a person in the public eye to receive threats. My greatest worry always was that someone might try to harm our children. These threats did not hamper my work at all, but they did cause me at times to limit the activities of our children. They were kept close to home and encouraged over and over to be careful.

Each traumatic incident pertaining to my race or gender has marked an important turning point in my life. On these occasions, I have grown with pain, looked ahead rather than back, made new paths, rather than traverse old ones. Different people respond to discrimination with different styles. When facing disappointment due to race and gender, mine was always a response rather than a reaction.

In responding to discrimination, it is important to know yourself, who you really are, and to use the style we are most comfortable with to respond. But it is important to respond, if for no other reason than to counteract the pain. Otherwise, it can destroy you. Perhaps my own style in dealing with these situations has been unusual. It has never been my style to dwell on disappointment, even as a young child and even in later years, when perhaps it would have been helpful to others for me to pause and talk about disappointments. Instead, my response is to design and move immediately to alternative ways of achieving the desired goal. I have always been a goal-oriented doer and am confrontational with a clear purpose. In responding to bias because of my race and gender in higher education administration, my experiences show that individual leaders can empower organizations and organizations can empower their leaders.

The best institution leaders with whom I have worked were those who could empower the whole enterprise as they empowered themselves. My main counsel to young professionals today: even with discrimination, which I am sure people from minority groups experience at some time in their lives, I encourage you to learn how to empower the situation beyond yourself and then you surely will rise to leadership positions, whether or not this is your initial goal.

My Many Sources of Strength and Support

My family, children, friends, and professional and other community organizations have been key sources of strength as I have functioned as a minority in higher education administration. This additional strength came primarily from their belief in me, their belief in my sense of values and fairness, and my ability to perform. Community service that has permitted me the opportunity to share with others, pool ideas and work in teams to solve problems, has been particularly helpful. Examples of my community service are my memberships in the American Association of Higher Education, the Education Testing Service, North Central Association Commission of Institutions of Higher Education, and the community and civil rights organizations I have assisted. The international lecture tours for the United States Information Agency (USIA) have been enabling to me and helped shape my perspective for responding to delicate situations in higher education administration. The church—a unique place for reflection—has always been an important factor in my life.

I have been helped by mentors of all races and both genders. Some have provided one-time or occasional help; others have advised me continually. Their encouragement has meant more than anything else. They include Derek Bok, Robert Atwell, Jack Peltason, Donna Shalala, Donna Shavlik, Hanna Gray, Russ Edgerton, Alfred S. Spriggs, Edith Thomas Dalton, Father Ted Hesburgh, Father Timothy Healy, David Gardner, Ann Reynolds, Martha Church, Lewis Bodi, Milton Bassin, Ole Kleppa, Thelma Perkins, Sister Joel Read, George Armstrong, Florence Frazier, Pearlie Dove, Allan Ostar, Goerge Tate, Donald Stewart, Henry McBay, Patricia Thrash, Mary Thornton Phillips, Robert Gale, Greg Anrig, Norman Francis, the now deceased James P. Brawley, Vivian Henderson, Benjamin E. Mays, J. J. Dennis, and James McPheeters.

Messages for the Future: Maintaining a Strong Conscience for Dealing with Racism in Society

There were many sources of strength that sustained me as I dealt with racism, discrimination and bigotry in our society and in higher education institutions. The four sources of strength that I relied on the most are my fondness for my roots and the people who helped me overcome early obstacles in life; the encouragement and support I have received from family and friends; my passionate pursuits of social justice for the disadvantaged; and my eagerness to contribute to the betterment of all people.

I have also found inspiration from phrasing and quoting over and over some of the lessons I have learned from experience. I advise the reader to do likewise: phrase your lessons from life, and pass them on to others. It is pleasure to share lessons learned with others. These are some of mine.

On culture: "Be proud of your own culture, refer regularly to the sources of strength of those of the earlier generations, realizing that regardless of how difficult our problems, their difficulties were much greater than the ones we know today." Know your own culture, and read the literature.

On the pursuit of quality: As my grandmother used to say, anything worth doing is worth doing well. During my presidency of Metropolitan State, I challenged the institution to pursue quality by encouraging everyone to "make the pursuit of quality a way of life, not just a one-time event."

Whose world is it anyway? So often we hear others say that the world is a white man's world. I have always challenged this notion and encouraged the idea that it is not a white man's or white woman's world, not a black man's or black woman's world, not anybody's world all to themselves. Instead, this is a *shared* world, and it is your duty to help make it better for all. This is what our struggle is all about."

Looking Ahead: Helping to Strengthen America's Economy

My own personal experiences in resisting, and in some cases overcoming, the effects of racism, bigotry, and discrimination show me clearly how these problems erode America's economy and limit the greatness of our country. Leadership in America, at all levels of organizations, can do something about this issue!

In our public today, in 1999, we have a deep reservoir of good will, as shown by many different people of different races. Can leaders tap this good will? Can leaders inspire the public to use this good will for the common good, as so many in the public want to do? Can we bring people together? Can we work together? Can we live together? To me, this is the issue for higher education leaders to think about today as they guide their campuses to a state of greater racial harmony where people feel good relating to each other. There is more at stake for all of the country than just the benefits to a particular campus.

Much has been achieved by changing the laws to bring about improved civil rights, and a lot of laws have been changed. Much of the remaining work to be done depends on economic empowerment of the disadvantaged and how leaders execute their roles in colleges, universities and all other organizations. Leaders must set the tone and bring reassurance to their employees and to the public that will motivate individuals to work voluntarily for social progress and racial harmony. Managers must change the status quo within organizations and keep on changing it.

There are special reasons why leadership should be concerned about effects of discrimination today. The two most important reasons relate to the rights of individuals and the need to have a competitive economy. The most important reason for the elimination of racism, bigotry, and discrimination is that everyone is entitled to just and fair treatment. But also important is the fact that the elimination of these problems will increase the productivity of individuals and organizations and thus improve the American economy.

Just suppose we can reduce racism, bigotry, and discrimination and increase our economic productivity by five percent on the average. What a change this would cause to our national economy! I believe that the development of our human resources, and fair treatment of all people regardless of their race and gender are the best, and perhaps cheapest, ways to strengthen America's economy.

Racism, bigotry, discrimination, and prejudice are clear impediments to our country's competitiveness in a global economy. They lessen people's productivity and cause more errors at work; people are not as creative as they have the potential to be because they are distracted from the task at hand.

To be effective, leaders in higher education today must think about the needs of their own institutions and then join with other leaders in American society to help deal with the consequences of racism and discrimination for the whole country.

From Cotton Picker to University CEO

CHARLIE NELMS

The offspring of subsistence farmers, I grew up on a small farm in the Delta region of Arkansas surrounded by mega cotton plantations, where segregation was the law of the land. I was the fifth of eleven children. My siblings and I, like most African American youth of that era, attended a one-room country school where one poorly prepared and inadequately paid teacher was expected to teach upwards of one hundred students in preprimer through the sixth grade.

Like most states throughout the South, Arkansas operated under the split school year until the mid-1970s. Under the split-year concept, blacks chopped cotton from late spring through the middle of July and attended school for about six weeks in July and August, at which time school closed for the cotton picking season. School resumed after the crop was harvested, which was usually around Thanksgiving. Of course, if the harvesting process had been delayed by unfavorable weather conditions it meant that school was sparsely attended although officially opened. (White children attended school continuously from September through May.) It should be noted that the school board was comprised of plantation owners and local white businessmen.

Noted for its abject poverty on the one hand and its staunch segregation on the other, the Delta region had a way of squelching the aspirations of even the most motivated, intelligent, and sanguine. Determined not to let the conditions of poverty nor the prevalence of racism destroy their dreams, my parents, neither of whom had completed elementary school, instilled in my siblings and me the belief that education has a transformative value that empowers one to improve not only his or her own life but the lives of African Americans and other disenfranchised people generally. To make sure that each one of their children completed high school and had the opportunity to

39

attend college, my parents mortgaged their forty-acre farm many times over, while suffering the indignities of racism.

Undergirded by the belief that my mission in life was to make life better for myself and others, I persisted through high school and entered college with the idea of earning a degree in agriculture and working for the Farmer's Home Administration. I thought this was the best avenue open to me for improving the quality of life for rural African Americans. However, this scenario simply was not to occur. My vision of how I might improve conditions for the better was greatly influenced by my participation in student government at the University of Arkansas at Pine Bluff and firsthand observation of the impact of legalized racism. At my alma mater the enrollment was 100 percent African American. The period of my matriculation was the 1960s, an era characterized by student demonstrations and the commitment to create a more equitable educational, economic, and social system. It was during this era, at twenty years of age that I decided that perhaps I could play a more significant role in reshaping the social fabric of America by becoming a college president. After all, I rationalized, America's colleges and universities are the places that educate this country's leaders. My goal was to become president of a historically black college or university. Despite what my parents had taught me about becoming anything that I wanted to become, I was not convinced that this meant being president of a white college. I am not sure they thought it either!

Today, as I reflect on the1960s and higher education's seemingly inane response to the problems that continuously beset us, I cannot help but wonder how life might have been improved for African Americans had more of our people taken jobs with the Farmer's Home Administration or, as school principals and superintendents, or if more of us had run for elective office.

Career Path

By nearly any definition or list of characteristics I consider myself to be a nontraditionalist. It only seems natural that my path to the chancellor's office has been anything but traditional. Unlike most university CEOs, I have never been a full-time faculty member, department chair, or dean. Unlike the majority of this country's presidents, I do not have a graduate degree in the arts and sciences or what is thought of as a traditional academic discipline. Influenced by the student demonstrations of the 1960s and the belief that colleges and universities were not responsive enough to student needs, I earned degrees in college student personnel and higher education administration. My decision to do so was predicated on the belief that an appreciation for the relationship between affective and cognitive development in students was critical to exercising effective executive leadership at the university level. In retrospect, my experience is supported by this belief.

Throughout my career I have succeeded in combining teaching and administration. In fact, except for three years spent as vice-president for student services at a community college, I have always requested and received a combined teaching and administrative appointment. My most memorable time as a teacher was when I had the opportunity to work with a group of students at Earlham College, a Quaker liberal arts institution, where I designed several courses that sought to educate students in the most holistic sense possible. The courses focused on topics such as education and racism, conflict resolution, global nutrition and hunger, black and white relations, values clarification, and a host of other topics. I experienced personal growth and joy in team teaching these courses with students and other faculty. Despite my nontraditional teaching experience, I earned tenure as a faculty member at a different institution in 1981. However, it should be noted that the tenure decision was a controversial one with significant racial overtones. While my academic division recommended that I be granted tenure and promoted to the rank of associate professor, the recommendation of the dean for academic affairs was negative. Both the dean and the acting chancellor attempted to persuade me to withdraw my request for promotion and tenure. Believing that I had earned tenure and promotion, based on my accomplishments, I refused to withdraw my request. The dean's negative decision notwithstanding, I was granted tenure, but I was not promoted. Shortly after being informed that this action was affirmed by the Indiana University Board of Trustees, I resigned to accept the position of vice president for student affairs at Sinclair Community College. Ironically, three and one-half years later I returned to Indiana University as professor of education and chancellor of the East Campus in Richmond.

Career Development Strategies

Although my career path has been nontraditional when compared to that of many other university CEOs, I have always placed three questions above every other consideration, including money, when deliberating whether to pursue a particular position. First, will I be able to make a difference? Second, will I be able to do more than meet the responsibilities outlined in the position description? Third, will I get trapped in the institution or position?

Although the expectation may not have been there in my various positions, I have always made time for professional development. Often at a great sacrifice to my family, I have written and published articles, participated in national meetings, served on state and national boards, made speeches, and served as a consultant to nonprofit agencies, colleges, and universities. For the five years prior to becoming a university CEO, I averaged approximately a dozen presentations of various sorts per year. Since initially becoming a

CEO in 1987 I have had as many as twenty-five professional development engagements or speeches per year. The articles that I have published in refereed journals and the presentations I have made at regional and national conferences have helped to buffer the criticism that often resonates in some academic circles about the inappropriateness of a background in student services for the presidency. Success as a teacher and scholar, no matter how nontraditional the teaching might be, forces citizens of the academic community to rethink many of their strongly held views about the ideal background of a successful college president. Such rethinking is long overdue.

Leadership Identification Program and Mentors

Contrary to popular belief, being talented is not enough to become a college CEO. One can be extremely talented and experienced, but unless others are aware of your talent and potential, one is unlikely to ascend to the presidency or to any significant position of leadership. Moreover, it is my contention that a good mentor combined with broad experience and participation in a leadership identification program increases significantly one's chances of becoming a university president.

My career has been spiced with a good mix of opportunity, timing, and luck! Luck because of the wonderful mentors that I have been privileged to have along the way. They have been female and male; white and black; old and young; opinionated and energetic. However, as different as they were, all of them took a personal interest in me, and each of them possessed four characteristics: they provided honest feedback; they challenged me to think and respond creatively; they served as a conduit to information; and they helped me gain a greater edge than might otherwise have been the case. Perhaps the one mentor who has had the greatest impact on my life is a man who has spent the better part of four decades developing African American talent in Arkansas: Dr. Lee Allen Torrence, a professor at the University of Arkansas at Pine Bluff. Torrence, as he is affectionately known by his students, had a way of challenging one to keep things in perspective, to think strategically and holistically. Above all, he challenged us to always remember that leadership is an opportunity for service to human kind generally but to the African American community in particular.

Two other mentors, both Caucasians, provided immeasurable support during the early stages of my career. The first was the late Dr. August Eberle, a professor at Indiana University, my major professor and doctoral thesis advisor. A tall, gruff-speaking man with a military appearance, Eberle had a way of giving a push when one was stalled or a pat on the back when one was down. I recall him ripping the first draft of my dissertation to shreds, but the next week he encouraged me not to let his criticism get in the way of what I needed to do! Between 1970 and his retirement in 1979, Dr. August Eberle mentored over two dozen African American graduate students enroute to the doctorate in higher education administration. At a memorial service for Dr. Eberle four years ago, his widow honored me greatly by asking me to be one of the speakers.

Another mentor who had a profound impact on my professional development was Danilo Orescanin, professor of business at Indiana University and former chancellor of Indiana University Northwest. It was Dan Orcescanin who supported my nomination for the American Council on Education Fellows program in 1981 and my candidacy for the chancellor's position at Indiana University East in 1987. During my ACE fellowship year, Dan permitted me to join him at various budget and planning meetings with the president of the university and members of his cabinet. Concerned about the chancellor's salary when offered the position at IU East by the president of the system, Dan was the person on whom I called on for advice on how best to proceed, since I did not want the president to think that I was more concerned with the financial incentives of the position than the opportunity it afforded. As one of the three Indiana University system vice-presidents, Dan pursued my concern with the president, and a modified offer was forthcoming.

I have had the opportunity to participate in three leadership identification programs, each of which positively impacted my life in different ways. Through the Ford Foundation, I had the opportunity to pursue doctoral studies at Teachers College, Columbia University in the early 1970s, an era when some Caucasians truly thought they could make a difference and were not threatened by the achievements and presence of African Americans. After leaving Columbia in 1973, without a doctorate, I had the opportunity to complete my studies at Indiana University under the Lilly Endowment's Intern Program in Higher Education. As a Lilly intern I spent the year working in the office of the dean for academic affairs at Indiana University—Purdue University at Indianapolis. This opportunity represented my first real foray into academic administration. The third opportunity took the form of the American Council on Education Fellows program in 1981–82. Although it was strongly suggested by the program's director that my professional aspiration of wanting to become a college president was farfetched, given the background of most college presidents, I was accepted into the program and had a positive experience as assistant to the vice-president of academic affairs at Roosevelt University in Chicago.

The ACE Fellows program probably had a much greater impact on my ascendancy to the chancellor's office than either the Ford or Lilly programs for several reasons. First, the ACE Fellows experience came much later in my career. Second, the fellows program helped to legitimize my experience in academe, which is very important when one considers my student services background. Finally, the fellows program provided access to a potentially powerful and useful network.

Positions Held Prior to Presidency

After looking at my resume the casual observer may erroneously conclude that I am a job hopper because I have had seven different jobs in
significantly different institutions during my twenty-year tenure in academe.
Quite the contrary. Each of the positions that I have held and each institutional setting in which I have worked was chosen deliberately. Positions that
I have held include ombudsman for student affairs; counselor and lecturer in
education; assistant admissions director; associate dean for student development; associate academic dean; director of university college; and vice-
president for student services. Each of these positions afforded me the
opportunity to work directly with students, and the opportunity to interface
with faculty and administrators and to work closely with the community.
Each position gave me the opportunity to test ideas and concepts, to design
and implement numerous programmatic initiatives, and to push myself to the
limits of my energy and creativity.

Among the positions that I have held, two stand out as being particularly
useful in preparing me for the chancellorship. As ombudsman for student
affairs at the University of Arkansas at Pine Bluff from 1968 to 1970 I had
the opportunity to view the university from close range, an opportunity un-
paralleled by any before or since. I had the opportunity to see how the inertia
and bureaucratic red tape interferes with progress. Moreover, I had the opportunity to see who really controls the power in academe and to discern the
difference between good institutional management on the one hand and effective leadership on the other. In my view, management is more a matter of
technique and doing things right, while effective leadership draws on one's
values, creativity, the willingness to take risks and doing the right thing.

My primary role as ombudsman was to be an advocate for students and to
help them solve problems in the most expeditious manner possible. This undertaking offended a lot of people along the way. However, the position provided
unlimited access to the president of the university, to other executive-level
administrators, and to faculty. I gained an immense appreciation for the potential power of the presidency, as well as the power of *passive resistors* who may
have disagreed with the action requested by the president. I left the position
with a better understanding of the relentless pressure that the president is sub-
jected to in attempting to balance the competing desires and needs of various
university constituencies without violating his or her own value system.

Just as the ombudsman position provided an overview of the university
administration and a glimpse of the presidency, the position of associate dean
for academic affairs and director of university college at Indiana University
Northwest, perhaps the most urban university campus in Indiana, enabled me
to experience the politics of education and the leadership constraints in such
an environment. Although the university is located in Gary, Indiana, it was

not a *part* of the city to any significant degree. In fact, many students, faculty, and administrators alike seemed to take pride in the fact that the campus was called IU Northwest rather than IU Gary. (There was even talk in some campus circles of moving the university south to the town of Merrilville, Indiana.) The institution's name might seem like a subtle issue, but it was a significant factor in a region of the state with more than sixty different ethnic groups, a region where discrimination in housing and other areas was rampant. For the first time in my life, I found myself working with people, many of whom would rather have been employed at a research or residential campus than at a regional campus, where the mission was to serve working people. For the first time in my professional career I found myself working among people who seemed oblivious to their sexist and racist tendencies. For the first time in my professional career I experienced a head-on collision with protectors of the status quo under the guise of faculty governance and academic standards. When it came time for promotion and tenure, I found myself not only having to defend my scholarly work, but also my extensive community involvement with the school system, Urban League, United Way, and various social service agencies. My activities represented exactly those attributes in which I thought a faculty member or administrator at an urban university should be engaged.

In summary, it can be said that I came of age politically at Indiana University Northwest. I became more observant and more guarded with my ideas and thoughts. I became more political and more determined to do what is right and in the best interest of students and the communities served by the university. The one lesson learned from my IU Northwest days that I find still applicable today is that as a leader, *it is more important to be respected than to be liked.*

Awareness of the Presidency

Contrary to what many incumbent presidents would have one believe, becoming a college or university president depends on *more* than merit. While academic and professional credentials are important, being *connected* to the right people is equally as important. While there is not necessarily anything unethical or illegal about being in the right network, since most African Americans and women have not been a part of such networks historically, they have been excluded from serious consideration for the presidency. Most search committees and boards of trustees welcome applications from minorities, but fewer committees invite minority applicants for interviews, and only a handful of trustee boards actually appoint minority persons as presidents.

Formally, I became aware of the first chancellor's position that I held through an advertisement in the *Chronicle of Higher Education*. As a former

ACE Fellow I requested and received a nomination from the director of the fellows program. Informally, however, I became aware of the position and how my candidacy might be received approximately eighteen months before the position became vacant or was advertised. The feedback came from a highly respected professor, researcher, and administrator who had taken a personal interest in my career advancement prior to his retirement from the Bloomington campus in 1980. Since I had worked on the Northwest campus of Indiana University for six years there were many people at Indiana University, including the president and members of his cabinet, who were familiar with my work. While I do not mean to suggest that my experience was not a significant factor in my selection, I am astute enough to recognize that my professional and personal connection to Indiana University was valuable in the final outcome. Since my appointment as chancellor represented a first for African Americans, I suspect that my connection to the university took on even greater significance. From almost any perspective, I was considered a safe prospect with a record of success. I contend that I was a safe prospect because the university's central level administrative group was familiar with my professional accomplishments and comfortable with my leadership and communication style. My approach to effective communication is to be direct and to-the-point, but to avoid attacking people on a personal level.

The Interview Process and Initial Response

"Ladies and gentlemen thank you for joining us for lunch today as we continue the process of selecting a chancellor for Indiana University East. It is anticipated that the committee will complete its work and forward a recommendation to the president of the university by mid-April. We have conducted the search in accordance with the university's affirmative action policy, and Dr. Nelms is our first candidate . . ."

The introductory comments from the chairperson of the chancellor's search committee underscored the importance of language and how different people hearing the same words perceive things differently. Except for a lone African American male, the luncheon gathering consisted of about twenty-five Caucasians, all of whom were males except two. For me, the chairperson's comments unwittingly communicated that Charlie Nelms is our affirmative action candidate; while for him it probably meant that the university had followed its own policy with respect to open searches and that I was the first to be interviewed. My speculation, during and subsequent to the interview and my appointment, is that for many people my appointment was for affirmative action purposes. My fervent belief is that

I was appointed because I was the best candidate for the position and I had a connection to Indiana University.

I sensed, from questions during the campus interview, that some of the persons present expected me to possess special insights into the issues surrounding minority student and faculty enhancement beyond possessing a sensitivity to the need to extend opportunities to underrepresented groups. Some of the persons present seemed to want a savior, while others wanted me to enumerate a specific action plan. The best part of the selection process involved discussions with the incumbent president of Indiana University and the person who had been named to succeed him. In both instances I had direct discussions with them about the potential reaction to my appointment without dwelling on the topic. I learned from those discussions that some people at Indiana University East and elsewhere in the university had questioned whether the city of Richmond was ready for an African American chancellor. I was heartened by what the president told me his response had been: "If we wait until the community is ready, we may never make an appointment. I must do what is right for the university." Moreover, he indicated to me, "I have concluded that you are the best person for the position, and you just happen to be black." Throughout my tenure as chancellor I have never felt that support from the president or the trustees was influenced in any way by my race. The president and the trustees were very supportive of me, both personally and professionally.

Initial Response to Appointment

The announcement of my appointment and subsequent arrival on campus proceeded in a predictable fashion. There were lots of smiles and congratulatory notes, the usual speculation about the chancellor's reorganization plans, advice about who to *look out* for, community people who called or stopped by to wish me well and to tell me how great my predecessor was! To make certain that members of the local country club did not respond negatively to the application from their first black prospect, my nomination was spearheaded by three of the community's most prominent businessmen. Similarly, the leading real estate company in town assigned their best agent to work with my family to secure housing. Except for one major snafu, the local newspaper coverage was quite positive and laudatory about my previous stay in the community and my association with Earlham College. The snafu occurred when a local newspaper reporter, in attempting to be humorous, admonished local drivers not to mistake me for one of the possums along a particular street that I was known to use for jogging! I later learned that the possum reference caused quite a stir at the newspaper and earned the reporter a verbal reprimand.

Circumstances that Occurred Following My Appointment

After being named chancellor of Indiana University East, numerous incidents occurred that reflected varying degrees of ignorance at best or racism
at worst. However, many of my Caucasian colleagues would describe me as
being over-sensitive. I have found it rather common for many Caucasians,
unable to defend their racial insensitivities, to blame the victim. After all,
they rationalize, "You have a problem, not us!" What follows are four examples of incidents that occurred involving a subordinate, a chancellor colleague from another campus, and a prominent supporter of the campus and
faculty.

Approximately two weeks prior to assuming my duties in 1987 I held a
meeting with members of the campus' executive council (administrators who
report directly to the chancellor) whereupon I shared in a professional and
sensitive manner my thoughts about the importance of teamwork, and internal communications, my preference for honest feedback rather than people
telling me what they think I want to hear, and my belief that professional
people can disagree without being disagreeable.

Like any new CEO, early in my tenure I reviewed the campus budget
with an eye toward making some minor adjustments to address several things
that I considered to be important, but which had not been adequately considered when the budget was prepared. I shared my plans with the vice chancellor for administrative affairs, who proceeded to give me a lecture on the
budget process and the inappropriateness of the proposed adjustments and
how my plans were not in keeping with university policies and guidelines.
When I asked him to provide me with copies of the policies in question and
he could not do so, it became clear that he was pursuing his own agenda. Had
I been white I do not feel that the vice chancellor would have challenged me,
especially in such an aggressive manner. At this point, I had a decision to
make, which was to confront the situation head-on or to spend the remainder
of my tenure being second-guessed and challenged by a subordinate. I chose
the former course of action. I calmly looked my colleague squarely in the eye
and told him that I was chancellor and as long as I had presidential approval
of my plans his thoughts about the appropriateness of my decision did not
matter. Moreover, all I needed him to do was to follow through on the request. That was the first and only time that I received such a lecture from a
subordinate during my tenure as chancellor!

Another incident relates to the review process that Indiana University's
president, chancellors, and system-level vice presidents are required to un-
dergo during the fifth year of their appointment. During the 1991 through
1992 academic year, the president of Indiana University and three chancellors
were scheduled for review. The committee to review the chancellor is appointed by the president of the university with nominations from the Univer-

sity Faculty Council, a university-wide faculty governance body. Although the committee is comprised primarily of faculty, other representatives include students, nonfaculty employees, and community people. Chaired by a senior faculty member from the IU East campus, the evaluation committee appointed to evaluate my performance consisted of eleven people.

After waiting for approximately eight weeks following the committee's appointment and having not heard from the chairperson about the procedures the committee planned to utilize and what my role in the evaluation process would be, I prepared and sent to the chairperson a comprehensive self-appraisal of my performance. In the transmittal memorandum I offered to meet with the committee and encouraged the members to review my annual reports, remarks from my annual state-of-the campus addresses, and any other relevant data. While there was not a direct acknowledgement of receipt of my self-appraisal report, I learned from my executive assistant that the committee chair had requested that copies of my annual reports and speeches be placed on reserve in the library. My assistant complied with this request.

Somewhat anxious, although confident of my accomplishments, I inquired of two chancellors from other campuses about the progress in their review. Each person described a process that was significantly different from my own, one in which they were significantly involved, which prompted me to raise questions with the president of the university about the absence of university-wide guidelines for such reviews. In fact, I told him that I thought the process was so fraught with problems that the final report would not accurately reflect the challenges that I had faced or my accomplishments as chancellor. Consequently, the committee's recommendations would not be as useful as they might otherwise be. The president acknowledged my suggestion that guidelines were needed and attempted to reassure me that the quality of my work was known and appreciated by him and by everyone else. While I am confident that the president's response was genuine, I am not sure that he ever fully grasped the depth of my concern about the process or with what I interpreted as a lack of respect by the committee. No matter how supportive the president's comments were, I could not ignore the fact that my predecessor had been actively involved in his five-year review.

Five months after the committee was appointed, I received a draft of the committee's report with the request to meet with the committee to share my reactions to the report. To say that I was irate would be an understatement. My anger turned to pain, given the extent to which I had devoted myself to helping the institution to achieve its goals, yet my review had been handled in such a callous manner. Later my anger and pain turned to a calm and a focused response to some of the inferences contained in the report. Among the committee's positive findings were the following: the chancellor is universally viewed as providing excellent leadership for IU East; listens very well; is supportive of faculty professional development; displays kindness, genuineness, and sincerity in his leadership; and offers sensitive leadership in the effort to reduce racial discrimination in the community. Conversely, the committee reported a wide range of *perceptions* purportedly held by *some* members of the campus community. Some of these included the perception that "he interferes with middle management and does not allow subordinates to do their jobs; has a tendency to take offense and harbor grudges over perceived policy disagreements; and circumvents procedures in order to get a priority item of his resolved." The committee also reported that I am perceived as circumventing the university's affirmative action guidelines.

Since the committee had made it clear that the purpose of the meeting with me was to get my reaction to the draft report rather than to discuss the content, I deemed it appropriate to prepare a written response to the report and I requested that my response be attached to the committee's report. In my written response and during the meeting with the review committee I expressed my disappointment with the process and challenged the committee to substantiate some of the inferences of inappropriate behavior on my part or delete them from the report. To refute the committee's notation that some members of the campus community perceived the number of female administrators as having declined under my leadership I provided data which showed a 53.5 percent increase in the percent of female administrators. In its final report the only thing the committee changed was to add the phrase "female academic administrators" which they alleged really represented what they meant. Even so, the supposed clarification too was false!

Was the process used to conduct my review influenced by the fact that I am African American? I have asked myself that question many times over and concluded that it was. Additionally, I concluded that the lack of respect accorded me throughout the review process and the perceptions contained in the report reveal a basic mistrust of African American leadership and the resistance of some in academe to that leadership. If the review process was not influenced by race, I must say that I find it a strange coincidence that my review was handled so differently from that of my colleagues on other campuses. I sense that some members of the university community believe that I am intruding on their turf when I move beyond the realm of simply acquiring the physical and fiscal resources needed by the campus.

Two other experiences that were equally as troubling involved a discussion in 1990 between myself and a chancellor colleague from another Indiana University campus about the approaching session of the Indiana General Assembly and speculations about how successful the various campuses were likely to be in increasing their appropriation. My colleague turned to me and proclaimed with great certainty that he was confident that I would be successful. When I asked if he knew something that I did not know he responded, "Let's face it Charlie, you are a minority." The implication clearly was that the Indiana General Assembly somehow would be more influenced by my race than by my ability to make a legitimate case for increased support based on campus needs. That comment modified permanently the relationship that existed between that colleague and me. Sadly, he continued to see me as his chief competition.

The final example that I will share here came from a prominent Richmond citizen and university supporter. As a part of the overall lobbying effort for increasing higher education funding in Indiana, every two years the presidents of Indiana University and Purdue University host luncheon meetings for business and civic leaders at a dozen or more sites around the state. In 1990, Richmond was the site of such a luncheon with over two hundred people in attendance. As the local host, I was busy greeting guests as they arrived and thanking them for accepting our invitation. Later that afternoon, following the event, I received a telephone call from a person in attendance. He began by saying that he had debated whether to share a matter with me that came up at his table during lunch since the person who made the statement is a strong supporter of the campus and of me as well, or so he thought. When one of his tablemates, an out-of-town visitor, inquired who I was, the response from a major campus supporter was, "He's the head nigger in charge!"

While I do not know whether the situations referenced above reflect what other African American presidents at predominantly white universities have encountered, I do know that they represent four examples that were taken from a list of approximately twenty such circumstances that I have encountered over a five-year period. My concern is not with the number of such circumstances, but with the fact that they thrive in an academic environment that purportedly advocates cultural and ethnic diversity, equity, excellence, and all the other laudable values that educators are prone to articulate so eloquently.

Lest one conclude that the life of an African American CEO at a predominantly white university is a curse of the worst magnitude, it is equally important when talking in detail about some of the challenges of African American leadership on predominantly "white" universities to discuss the genuinely kind, supportive, and well-meaning people with whom I work that make going to work a challenging and rewarding experience.

Reaction and Reflection

My reaction to each of the race-related situations encountered throughout my career generally and as chancellor at Indiana University East in particular has consistently reflected emotions ranging from anger to pain, followed by a specific plan of action for confronting the situation head-on. In almost all cases, my Caucasian colleagues and superiors have interpreted these situations differently than I have. Without failure, they seem to be able to rationalize away the racist behavior of a colleague while failing to understand my reaction! In comparing notes with colleagues from other universities, I find my experience is not unique. Indeed, every African American CEO with whom I am acquainted has his or her own horror stories to tell.

Probably the most important lesson learned from my encounters is how little *true* progress has been made in the racial sensitivity of many whites since my adolescent days in the Delta region of Arkansas. Racism of that era was blatant and overt and supported by state and federal legislation, and it was on constant display. The signs declaring "colored" and "white only" have been replaced by discipline-specific admissions requirements developed by racially insensitive faculty that have the effect of keeping African American students out of certain disciplines. Twenty-five years ago, small groups of faculty and administrators did all of the interviewing and hiring. Today we have search and screen committees that make the same kinds of decisions that groups of yesteryear made, only now those decisions are made under the guise of excellence.

On a personal level, I have learned that to survive and be successful as an administrator in a predominantly white university African Americans must have a well-developed sense of who they are and the capacity to form alliances with those who have a sense of fairness and are receptive to change; be willing to challenge the "status quo" rather than behaving like "tokens"; choose their fights carefully; conserve and use their energy wisely; keep their sights focused on the "big picture"; find satisfaction in their work, and not rely upon others for compliments. Above all, stay close to God and their families.

The Degree of Racism in American Institutions

Racism is not only alive and well in American institutions of higher education, but it is flourishing! Unfortunately, since much of the racism in academe is not of the vicious and blatant variety, it is often not recognized, let alone challenged by people of goodwill. Academic racism is cloaked under the guise of academic freedom, excellence, faculty governance, and peer review. It is undergirded by an arcane tenure system that provides a haven for the perpetrators of racism.

In order for persons who occupy university CEO positions to be effective in successfully confronting racism, they need three primary weapons: (1) a mandate from the board of trustees to design and implement an aggressive program to educate faculty and staff; (2) authority and resources to hire department chairs, directors, and deans with the fortitude to stand up to the perpetrators of racism with the confidence that they will be supported; and finally (3) the willingness of the state legislature to base the university's appropriation, in part, on its success in hiring and retaining African American faculty and staff and graduating African American students.

Impact of the Position on My Personal Life

The position of chancellor has had a profound impact, not only on my life but on the life of my family as well. First and foremost, is the loss of one's personal identity. Unfortunately, one becomes an extension of the position. In a small town such as Richmond, Indiana, the position of chancellor is customarily a high profile position, and it is made even higher because of my race and my commitment to community service. It was difficult, for example, to go out to eat or to a social event without people wanting to engage me in a conversation about some aspect of the university. I often compare my work to that of a person running for political office, except there is never an election! Being asked to make speeches to all types of groups who see me as an example of a "successful" person who can serve as a role model and mentor is at times overwhelming. After eight years in such a position, I learned to pace myself a bit more effectively.

On a positive note, the position provided me with a platform to pursue ideas and programmatic initiatives that help people, whether they be minority youth or rural whites. Additionally, the position brought my family closer together as a unit. My wife and I support each other more and have come to treasure the time that we have together. Our everyday experiences provide an excellent forum for teaching our son important lessons ranging from materialism to politics and from multiculturalism to volunteerism.

What Higher Education Does to Reduce Racism in the Larger Society

The most important thing that the higher education community can do to reduce racism in the larger society is to get its own house in order. By that I mean that colleges and universities should move beyond espousing lofty views about affirmative action and equal opportunity and begin practicing those precepts. As educators of current and future citizens, universities must reconsider many of their restrictive notions about what it means to be educated and make some major modifications in the courses that make up the core curriculum. Given the increasingly ethnic, diverse, and global society in which we live, by not mandating that students take courses that advance their understanding and appreciation of other cultures, we are behaving in an intellectually irresponsible manner. Rather than cowering under pressure from groups such as the National Association of Scholars, who challenge the legitimacy of ethnic studies, women's studies, or any non-Western or non-European curriculum, universities should pursue with vigor their mission of educating students rather than simply training them in a narrow disciplinary sense.

Finally, the higher education community can help to reduce racism in the larger society through the hiring decisions that are made. If universities believe in equality and equity, this belief should be reflected in the faculty, staff, and administrative composition. A diverse university work force is important not only for the purpose of providing African American students with greater opportunities, but for providing white students with role models who are African American. They need to see that African Americans are just as intelligent, articulate, and compassionate as whites. If white students see African Americans primarily in athletic and entertainment roles, they may erroneously conclude that this situation represents the extent of the abilities of African Americans generally.

Concluding Observations

Affirmative Action

In our rapidly changing society I believe that higher education represents our best hope for creating a more just, responsive, and compassionate society. As educational enterprises, universities serve as guardians and developers of the nation's most important energy source, brain power. Universities must help to develop the parameters within which students and the larger society can engage in productive dialogue on such controversial and poorly understood topics as multiculturalism, political correctness, affirmative action, reverse discrimination, and the like. Such dialogue must be woven into the very fabric of what universities do, which is to teach students. Unless these poorly understood issues are addressed in a deliberate and sustained manner, the opportunity for leadership by African Americans in predominantly white colleges and universities is lessened even more in the long term.

Unfortunately, affirmative action is little more than a phrase in most institutions of higher education. How else could universities continue to be such segregated places? Affirmative action is likely to continue to be an important phrase displayed on the bottom of university stationary or in job advertisements unless the federal and state governments hold institutions accountable for their employment practices. Funds should be withheld from universities that show no increase in the enrollment of African American students and the employment of African American faculty and administrators over a reasonable period of time. Moreover, trustees should evaluate the CEO on his or her success in helping the institution to meet its affirmative action goals.

Mentoring and Contending with Charges of Tokenism and Raiding

As an ardent supporter of the concept of mentoring I spend an enormous amount of time mentoring junior colleagues at my own institution as well as persons throughout the nation. In some instances, the relationship is long-term, while in others it may mean spending time conferencing on the telephone, scheduling time for a face-to-face discussion, or reading a paper or thesis proposal. I consider mentoring as one way of repaying a debt to people who have mentored me throughout my career.

Being called a "token" by other African Americans is painful, but it is also one of the realities of being the CEO of any predominantly white institution, whether it is a university or a business. However, being called a "token" and behaving like a token are two different things. There are numerous ways for the truly committed African American CEO to demonstrate that although his or her appointment may have been for symbolic reasons, he or she is not just a symbol. Involvement in the life of the African American community, hiring decisions, and the allocation of resources to address the needs of African American people and other underrepresented groups are significant ways that a CEO has of responding effectively to charges of tokenism from other African Americans. In other words, one can demonstrate that you are not a token by letting one's actions do the talking.

The raiding of historically black institutions by predominantly white institutions for faculty members and administrators is never acceptable no matter how laudable the reasons might be. A far more acceptable approach, in my view, is for white universities to form alliances and partnerships with historically black institutions. There are two strategies that I believe hold considerable promise. The first is the implementation of a faculty and administrative exchange program between the two sets of institutions. Such a program would expose African Americans to opportunities in a predominantly white institution while the white institution would have the benefit of an African American scholar or administrator from whom students and others in the university might learn a great deal. The gains from such an exchange program are mutual, but short-term at best.

The second strategy is to enlarge the pool of potential African American faculty and administrators by admitting and helping more African American graduate students to succeed in graduate schools. One part of the strategy would be for institutions of higher education from the two sectors to identify African American students when they begin college and enter into a pact whereby those who earn a baccalaureate degree with a grade point average of B or better will receive a free graduate education if they wish to pursue a collegiate teaching career.

Responsibilities of African American Academicians to the African American Community

The stress of contending with the rigors of life in academe notwithstanding, the extent to which African American academicians share their talents and time with the community will determine in large measure whether the masses of African Americans succeed in life. African American academicians must be willing to engage in applied research and adolescent African Americans must be able to see them in action, whether it is as a researcher or a volunteer. Although many African American academicians may physically move out of the community, they should never *move away* from the community.

The availability of support or interest groups for African Americans is just as appropriate as the formation of women's groups, disciplinary or honors organizations, fraternities or sororities. The only difference with African American support groups and what makes them unacceptable to many in academe, is that they are for a specific race. In addition to the usual challenges in academe, I believe that African American people have some challenges that are unique to them by virtue of their being minorities in a majority culture. The formation of such interest groups would in all probability not be understood or viewed in a positive light by white colleagues. Consequently, to the extent possible, the members of the interest group should attempt to communicate, as clearly as possible, the objectives of the group. Experience teaches me that fear and ignorance are two of the greatest threats to racial understanding and sensitivity. If the presence of such support groups will help its members to be successfully retained by the university, how can one afford not to be supportive? I believe that such organizations actually may be needed by whites who work in a majority African American environment.

I believe that the single most effective strategy that students have at their disposal is the pressure that they can place on trustees and presidents of colleges and universities to pursue worthwhile initiatives. As the primary constituent group for whom the institution exists, students can be effective change agents if they choose to use their power in the struggle for equality in higher education. In addition, students can put pressure on the governor and others who appoint trustees to make certain that trustee boards are more diverse and more sensitive to the importance of appointing African Americans to senior-level administrative positions.

The most important action that predominantly white institutions can take to increase the numbers of African American senior-level administrators is to get serious about affirmative action. By getting serious, I mean taking responsibility for helping to expand the pool of applicants by appointing African Americans to faculty and junior-level administrative positions, thereby insuring that they have the necessary credentials to be considered for senior-level administrative positions at a later time in their careers.

CHAPTER 3

Succeeding as a Female African American President of a Predominantly White College

VERA FARRIS

The helping nature of higher education beckoned to me rather early in life. During my undergraduate years, my admiration and respect were drawn to the fascinating purveyors of scientific knowledge. Once I entered college at Tuskegee Institute, home of George Washington Carver, I met Howard P. Carter, Dr. J. H. M. Henderson, and Norma Gaillard, all scientists par excellence who were less known than Dr. Carver, but who were even more influential to me. On the outside, I probably appeared to be a somewhat scruffy, homely, and very impoverished person. But my test scores and scholarships must have encouraged my teachers to probe beyond my outward appearance. The science faculty combined the characteristic seriousness of natural scientists and teachers with a gift for sharpening the competency of the next generation. They worked with individual students and tried to develop character as well as intellect. The love, patience, and time they spent so lavishly on my learning science and research made me want to be like them, and since they had devoted their lives to higher education, that motivated me to investigate a similar pathway.

Upon joining the professorate after completing my undergraduate and graduate education, I moved up through the faculty ranks at a somewhat faster pace than usual. Whereas the usual span of time to earn tenure is six to seven years, I was able to do so two years after receiving a tenure-track appointment. I was promoted to full professor only five years after earning tenure—a much shorter time than the norm. My rapid ascension in the faculty ranks was related to frequent demonstrations of outstanding teaching ability.

While carrying out my classroom responsibilities, I received several outstanding teacher awards, including the Award for Highest Teacher Evaluation at State University of New York at Stony Brook, 1970 through 1971; Outstanding Teaching Award, State University of New York at Stony Brook, 1972; Black Excelsior Award (for outstanding teaching), State University of New York at Stony Brook, 1972; The Chancellor's Excellence in Teaching Award presented by Chancellor Ernest Boyer of the State University of New York, 1973; Alumni Association Award for Excellence in Teaching, State University of New York, Brockport, 1974; and Distinguished Teaching Award, State University of New York, 1980. My faculty experiences also permitted the opportunity to undertake research, some of which was published in various scientific journals.

Considering administration as a part of my career grew out of my years of service in faculty governance. Early in my teaching career I served on and chaired several standing committees of the Faculty Senate at the university where I was employed. Eventually I was elected to chair an important statewide committee which was given the job of writing the guidelines for the Educational Opportunity Program for the State University of New York (SUNY).

The chairpersonship of an active faculty senate committee, and especially of a statewide committee is an excellent training ground for administration, since success in chairing these committees involves learning an incredible amount of bureaucracy, logistics, politics, negotiation, and compromise strategies. Sometimes these skills seem just as important as the knowledge required for the committee's topics.

One episode involving the statewide committee illustrates the type of skills needed. During my second year as chair, we decided to develop a summer institute to provide opportunities for faculty to share their ideas and outcomes in the area of innovative teaching and counseling. In this manner, it would be possible to disseminate successful new teaching strategies rapidly throughout the system. As the chair of the committee, I was expected to perform the major share of organizing the institute, inviting keynote speakers, making travel and lodging reservations, advertising, and undertaking other conference activities, although the full committee made the initial decisions, which required the chair to exercise tact and diplomacy.

We named the conference The Institute for Innovative Teaching and Counseling. It was highly successful and was greatly praised by faculty and administrators for its timeliness and for its administrative efficiency. The demand for additional summer institutes was so immense that these institutes became annual events, and I continued to serve as the director of the institute and chair of the committee. Even though I soon was offered an administrative title and began a rapid ascent up the administrative ladder, the Faculty Senate continued to request that I serve as director of the institute. In fact, in 1980 the chancellor of the SUNY system bestowed upon me a Distinguished Service Award in honor of the creation and implementation of the Institute for Innovative Teaching and Counseling.

It was clear to me that the chairmanship of the statewide committee with the concomitant development and establishment of the Institute for Innovative Teaching and Counseling represented my first major foray into higher education administration, since it was during this period that I was offered my first official administrative position, dean of special projects, in 1970.

Likes and Dislikes

The most appealing attribute of higher education administration to me is the opportunity to get a task accomplished, especially since in our field the task usually has as its goal the acquisition or dissemination of knowledge which will continue to improve all humankind. The administrative role in undertaking a task involves the development of processes or policies to ensure the achievement of the goal. The battery of skills and talents necessary to achieve process/policy development includes leadership, persuasion, listening, communication, and team building. I find exercising these skills appealing.

Least appealing to me are the excessive demands on the president's time. Social affairs, travel, public speaking, keeping current on national topics, committee meetings, athletic events, sitting on boards of directors, attending conferences, fund-raising, and writing articles can take a considerable toll on one's time unless a major effort is expended to balance one's time and one's personal life.

In addition to time demands, there are hidden financial costs to being a college president. Rarely is the president appropriately compensated for travel or expenditures. Certain donations are expected, and attire can be expensive if the particular college is associated with "prestige." Another unappealing aspect of the college presidency is its conspicuousness. The president's daily life takes place in a fish bowl, with the community often making a sport of overtly watching and commenting on it.

I was never fortunate enough to participate in any leadership development programs, but one of the persons who served to help me understand administration was Dr. Albert Brown, then president of SUNY College at Brockport. He promoted me into three positions, culminating in the acting vice-president for instruction and curriculum/associate provost for academic affairs. Further, he often permitted me to serve in acting positions while senior-level administration positions were under search. This situation allowed me to see higher education administration from a variety of perspectives, both in Academic Affairs and in Student Services.

The strategy that I employed in each of the acting roles was to keep a daily log of activities and of my thoughts about the activities and to evaluate my accomplishments on a weekly basis to see if I should have made different decisions. I also held regular meetings with whichever constituents were under my purview. In addition to understanding the agenda for the meeting, I also tried to determine what factors would motivate the group and what decisions might discourage or paralyze the group. Once these parameters were known, it usually was possible to move rapidly forward to accomplish any specified goal, even though I was in an "acting" administrative role.

My career has been concentrated in two states—New York and New Jersey. I spent two years in administrative positions at two of the institutions in the State University of New York system, eventually advancing to the post of vice-provost for academic affairs at one of the institutions. From there I moved to the New Jersey State College system, first as vice-president for academic affairs at Kean College for three years, and then on to the presidency at Richard Stockton College.

Probably the most useful posts in preparing me for a college presidency were the deanships and academic vice-presidencies that I held, since these roles have the faculty as their primary constituency. Having a basic understanding of what it means to be a faculty member and how to work with and motivate faculty is an important asset for a president. My work as a dean served me very well in this regard. The academic vice-presidency was also a very important post because it augmented my knowledge of curriculum, personnel, and budgets and because it assisted me in learning to work with the other vice-presidents and to be sensitive to their constituents. I became aware of my current presidential position when the then-president of the college told me he planned to resign. Shortly thereafter, several faculty members made an appointment to see me and urged me to accept a nomination for the position.

After being picked as president of Richard Stockton College and assuming the position, the initial response from most segments of the campus community to my selection was one of "wait-and-see." Stockton had a large number of viable candidates for the presidency, even though it recently had experienced major power struggles between institutional constituencies and was in the throes of several legal disputes between those constituencies at the time I assumed office.

The procedures used in the presidential search indicated that the college was being somewhat cautious in the important undertaking of interviewing candidates. The Presidential Search Committee, composed largely of trustees but including faculty, staff, and students, interviewed the seven semifinalists at a hotel near the airport. Some of the final interviews were held in the college-owned "presidential home" located fifteen miles from the college, with the outgoing president occasionally serving as an active participant.

The reaction of a group of the faculty and of the teachers' union was interesting. Even though the faculty had representation on the formal Presidential Search Committee, it was apparent that these groups undertook their own independent "review." During the search process, I learned from colleagues from my previous colleges of employment that some Stockton faculty were calling to inquire about my background. Questions were raised by these faculty about my publication record because a publishing date on one paper was very early in my career. (The article was published in 1953 when I was an undergraduate.) Further, an arbitration decision regarding a personnel matter that had been under my purview was incorrectly interpreted. Anonymous negative comments about these and other issues were circulated at Stockton during the interview process. To the credit of these groups, when the truth about these matters was finally revealed, it was accepted. Nevertheless, none of these activities was undertaken with respect to the other finalists, none of whom was a minority group member.

The students seemed to be the most delighted with my selection as president by the Board of Trustees. Despite a rumor, laced with bias, that I went through college as an academically disadvantaged "educational opportunity" student, the members of the student government and the student body were respectful in their interactions with me. Perhaps the fact that I had been an active and visible vice president for academic affairs at a northern New Jersey college where I developed a reputation for being student oriented, was helpful in my relations with students.

The administrative organization at my institution was undergoing a controversial "changing of the guard" which was part of the subject of the legal dispute among the constituents. A brief period of respite was needed before this area could be assessed and the beginning of an administrative team formed. The administrators therefore greeted my presidential selection with "cautious pessimism."

The response of the local community, as judged through the news media, was one of interest and curiosity. The focus was on the novelty of the selection of a *female* president, since in 1983 there were still very few women college presidents on the national scene. The fact that the new president was also an African American gave rise to some comments about an "affirmative action" candidate.

Two factors appeared to serve as important buffers for me when I assumed the presidency. One element was the fact that, as a native of Atlantic City which is seven miles from Stockton, I had received my K through twelve education in New Jersey, and many of my teachers, family, friends, and classmates were still in the area. In addition, my previous role as the vice president for academic affairs had been at Kean College, which is in northern New Jersey. In fact, my arrival at Kean had been marked with a great deal of similar media interest, since in 1980 there were very few women or minorities in the role of academic vice president at colleges where the majority of students and faculty were white. The same situation was true when I was the top academic officer at the State University of New York at Brockport.

In the interviews during the presidential search process, the trustees raised several questions about my experience and issues related to race. Two examples of these questions were

1. We have a very serious policy on affirmative action (see attached) which states that 50 percent of all hires must be with affirmative action and 25 percent must be minorities. What are your ideas on implementing our policy?
2. Southern New Jersey often can be very conservative in its views about minorities. Are you prepared to live and work in this environment?

One of the outcomes of these early discussions was the realization that all of my career in higher education as a faculty member and later as an administrator had been conducted at colleges similar to Stockton, that is, predominantly white institutions. However, the other colleges were much larger than Stockton. Apparently, the members of the Stockton Board of Trustees had discussed among themselves the implications of selecting a female African American president to administer a college composed mainly of white faculty, students, and staff. The largest percent of each constituency was male. Further, the trustees certainly were aware that southern New Jersey has a reputation for being considerably more conservative on race issues and more "southern" in its flavor than cosmopolitan northern New Jersey. There have been several incidents which involved race or which had racial overtones during my tenure at Stockton. In each instance, the trustees' support was firm and unfaltering. As a body, they have never tolerated even a hint of racism toward the president.

Facing Up to Racism

In the case where the president combines more than one visibly observable physical characteristic which is associated with prejudice, sometimes it is difficult to determine accurately whether the motivation of a specific group's action is racist, sexist, or some other "ist." However, in a 1989 report, a nationally known consultant was hired by the Stockton faculty assembly to make recommendations about faculty governance, staffing, and personnel guidelines. In his report, he noted under the rubic of "Racial Tension" that "perceptions of significant sex discrimination, by way of contrast, do not appear to be nearly as widespread nor as deeply held" as racism. He also stated that this perception of racism is reinforced, in the eyes of the black faculty and staff, by what is seen as "vicious," "low," and "rentless" attacks (by some white colleagues) on the president.

There are two specific examples of actions which may have been influenced or affected by race on my campus.

Caricatures Related to the President

In early December 1985 a newsletter termed alternately "The Mad Hatter" and "Professor Trueheart" began circulating under the editorship of a former faculty union official. These newsletters had a "Dear Abby" format with alleged "letters" and "responses." The written materials had a mocking tone in regard to me and were often scurrilous, with frequent reference to hats, since I often wear hats.

The faculty group wrote three or so volumes of the newsletter (about six pages each) prior to designing a particularly chilling caricature, which consisted of my picture with a very distinctive bull's eye superimposed on the picture. On December 13, 1985, when people arrived on campus, these large, highly visible, and garish bull's eye pictures had been hung throughout the college's main buildings. Apart from the obvious racial prejudice that was communicated, the connotation of execution and/or assassination along with prejudice was also plain. In fact, the president of the Faculty Union wrote a letter to the entire Stockton community stating, "There is absolutely no place on this campus for the distribution of racist caricatures of the president of this institution. There is no cause including the elimination of the tenure quotas, that justifies metastasizing the cancer of racism."

Thereafter, no further copies of the newsletter, nor other hate mongering caricatures appeared in the public domain of the campus.

Prosecutor's Investigation

In April 1986, the office of the Atlantic County prosecutor initiated an investigation of alleged financial irregularities at Stockton State College, claiming to have in its possession documentary evidence of same. Three areas were investigated:

1. Stockton State College expenditures for official receptions.
2. A President's Fund checking account.
3. Travel reimbursements from two private boards on which the president served as director.

In a twenty-three-page report on September 19, 1986, to the Stockton Board of Trustees, the prosecutor set forth his findings of fact made as a result of his twenty-four-week investigation, which included three sessions of "aggressive interrogation" of the president. The prosecutor found that no factual basis existed for any further prosecution in any of the matters cited and completely cleared me.

It should be noted that in mid-August 1986, long before the completion of the prosecutor's investigation and before I or anyone could predict the outcome, I wrote a letter to the entire college community stating that I had done nothing wrong and that it was my intention to provide a copy of the prosecutor's report to each member of the college whenever the investigation was ended. Therefore, on September 19, the day the report was transmitted to the trustees, the trustees honored my request and distributed the prosecutor's report in its entirety to every member of the college community and to each constituency, internal and external to the college, including the chancellor, the Foundation Board, and other major organizations affiliated with the college.

In summary, it was clear that I had engaged in no criminal conduct. Beyond that obvious conclusion, it was unequivocally shown that none of my actions, which were all closely reviewed, even so much as suggested any administrative or ethical improprieties on my part and that, in the final analysis, I had not engaged in any wrongdoing whatsoever.

Once the prosecutor's investigation of alleged criminal activity was concluded, I immediately requested that the trustees launch their own investigation to determine if any administrative improprieties or unethical activities on my part had transpired. Further, I requested, before knowing the outcome, that the trustees' report be distributed to all members of the community whenever such investigation was completed. In my letter of request to the trustees, I stated that "in fairness" to me this incident should not be "perceived merely as a roust and political skirmish." I believed then, and do now, that had this investigation not been seriously and fully undertaken, the college collectively, and I, individually, would have remained the victims of an insidious, if not cruel and vicious, deed which sought to create damage.

On December 10, 1986, the trustees issued their report to the entire college community. The trustees' report also cleared the president unequivocally of any and all wrongdoing with regard to administrative or ethical activities. The trustees' report and subsequent biennial evaluation of the president in June 1987 stated:

> RESOLVED, that the result of the comprehensive evaluation of President Vera King Farris is the unanimous affirmation of the Board that she has discharged her duties and responsibilities as President of Stockton State College and as an acknowledged leader in the field of higher education with conspicuous distinction and merit; and be it further

RESOLVED, that the Board with its full support and confidence reappoints Vera King Farris as President of Stockton State College and through this Resolution wishes to communicate this decision to the public and the New Jersey Board of Higher Education.

Curious Happenings

Although neither the prosecutor nor the prosecutor's investigation were necessarily racist, the investigation itself appeared to create opportunities for race-related activities. For example:

Example 1: News Media

The local newspaper wrote numerous articles about the prosecutor's investigation as front-page news with banner headlines, with misleading and unattractive pictures and with degrading anecdotal dialogue. All of these lengthy articles appeared day after day, month after month, despite the fact that at no time was I charged by the prosecutor with any criminal activity.

The pictures were so unattractive that people wrote letters to the editor protesting this aspect of the investigation and demanding an apology from the newspaper for its obviously racist slanting of the story. It should be noted that even after the prosecutor's report was transmitted and circulated, the local newspaper never published an article drawing clear attention to the fact that I had been exonerated of any and all wrongdoing. Fortunately, the wide distribution of the prosecutor's report and the trustees' report throughout the college community and the articles in the student newspaper rapidly transmitted information to the greater community. Many local groups such as the NAACP, Jewish organizations, and Anti-Defamation League cited the news media's reporting of the investigation as examples of racism and prejudice in our community.

Example 2: Attorney General's Office

By statute, it is the duty of the attorney general, upon request of a state employee, to provide for the defense of any action brought against that employee on account of an act or omission in the scope of his or her employment. Further, the attorney general may provide for the defense of a state employee if he or she concludes that such representation is in the best interest of the state.

The statutes indicate that the attorney general may refuse to provide for the defense of an action if he or she determines that

1. the act or omission was not within the scope of employment; or
2. the act or the failure to act was because of actual fraud, willful misconduct or actual malice; or
3. the defense of the action or proceeding by the attorney general would create a conflict of interest between the state and the employee.

None of the "grounds for refusal to provide defense" applied to me. Moreover, all of the conditions enumerated under the attorney general's duty to defend state employees held true. Further, at no time was I ever charged with a crime by the prosecutor's office. Yet, the attorney general's office informed me that it would not defend me and advised me to hire legal counsel at my personal expense.

The cost of my legal defense for the extended period of investigations (April 1986 to December 1986) was very high. Given the relatively minor nature of the allegations (albeit blown out of proportion by the media), the lack of any charge whatsoever by the prosecutor's office and the amount of funds involved in the entire investigation, it is truly amazing that the attorney general's office refused to represent me. In fact, the cost of my personal legal fees exceeded by a factor of five the amount of money being investigated.

To date, no other New Jersey college president to my knowledge has been refused representation outright, without a legal basis, as I was. However, once the prosecutor's report had been received, the attorney general's office responded positively to the requests both by the Stockton State College Board of Trustees and by the chancellor of higher education that my expenses be refunded. Finally, in 1988, my lawyer was able to negotiate with the attorney general's office to repay my expenses at a ratio of seventy cents for every dollar I had spent. This was considered a *very* generous act on the part of the attorney general's office, and I was deeply appreciative to receive the payment.

Example 3: Hate Groups

Beginning in early September 1986, copies of an Aryan Brotherhood flyer containing racist and anti-semitic statements were distributed throughout the campus. This incident, along with the discovery of White Aryan Resistance newspapers intermingled among the student newspapers shortly thereafter, caused controversy on the campus. For several consecutive weeks, racist newspapers and hate literature appeared on the campus on a regular basis.

Stockton's official policy was stated: We do not wish to deny freedom of speech to anyone, but any outside literature must go through the proper channels, that is, the Office of Campus Activities and the Office of Administration and Finance.

Stockton was contacted by a northern New Jersey–based Ku Klux Klan with an official request to hand out their organization's literature in the campus buildings. Stockton replied that their request would need to be accompanied by an invitation from a bonafide host group or service organization at the college. The Klan took the matter to court, and after two years, a settlement was reached which permitted the Ku Klux Klan to distribute literature on the campus but not within any building.

The Klan did not choose to exercise this opportunity and thereafter ceased all correspondence with the college. However, as a result of the prosecutor's investigation and the distribution of literature by hate groups the Atlantic County/Stockton College Community Human Relations Coalition was formed. It represents twenty-five groups, including the National Conference of Christians and Jews, B'Nai B'rith, the Federation of Jewish Agencies, several local high schools, the Atlantic Community College, several synagogues and Protestant and Catholic churches, and several governmental agencies.

The coalition, with the assistance of the Anti-Defamation League and the NAACP, undertook research to determine if the Ku Klux Klan had distributed literature or attempted to come onto other campuses. It was determined that at the time, very few (only one other) campuses had been actively pursued by the Klan. The coalition believed that two major factors helped attract the Klan's attention to Stockton—(1) The bias shown by the local newspaper in its handling of the prosecutor's investigation of the college president and (2) the outstanding success the college had achieved under the leadership of an African American woman president, which refuted the statements in the Klan's racist literature.

Bigotry within American institutions of higher education often appears to reflect the state of bigotry in the nation. The recent national controversies involving issues of "diversity" and "minority scholarships" at colleges and universities tell a clear story. For example, the dispute over what, if any, is the appropriate role of diversity in the accreditation of a college embroiled every level of education up to, and including, the secretary of education. The dispute with respect to minority scholarships correspondingly generated extensive debate. In both cases, the debate went beyond the educational to the political arena. Perhaps neither of these topics in and of itself represents bigotry or racism, but the debate often reflected institutions and a public divided along racial and ethnic lines. It also served, on occasions, to isolate and stigmatize minority students who attend higher education institutions with the financial assistance of scholarships for educationally and economically disadvantaged individuals.

In many ways, the chief executive officer sets the tone for the college. However, when it comes to the issue of race or diversity, many CEOs do not like to take a stand because these topics rapidly can become no win situations. The majority of constituencies at a college or university are highly intelligent, well read, and very articulate individuals. In the case of faculty, many are not particularly interested in diversity or multiculturalism and see the entire situation as being outside the purview of classroom teaching and not within the scope of their research interests. Or, even if they are committed to diversity in the society at large, they may fail to perceive that some of the same problems of racism affect their own institutions, even their own colleagues. Furthermore, many well-intentioned faculty tend to believe that calling attention to the problem of racism exacerbates it further.

It is necessary to convince faculty leadership and student organizations that they have a stake in whatever social problems may exist and that it will be to their advantage to assist in devising ways to diminish racism. Institutions of higher education can produce the research and serve as laboratories for exploring and experimenting with strategies to address this problem. If these mechanisms succeed in a college or university, which is in essence a microcosm of society, they can succeed in the larger society. Many discoveries and technological advances have emanated from our institutions of higher education. I am hopeful that the academy can also produce the solution to this problem and provide a model of individuals living together in peace and harmony.

Policies and Procedures

A college must review frequently its policies and procedures to ensure that they are fair and equitable to all persons to whom they apply. In the case of affirmative action, for example, it is important to remember that racial ethnicity and gender are *characteristics,* which typically are not possible to obtain, as compared to credentials and *qualifications* to which any individual can aspire. Therefore, most colleges will agree that affirmative action can be an important tool as a *hiring* consideration along with the appropriate qualifications. However, most will agree also that affirmative action should not replace qualifications and should not be invoked as a basis for *retention* or *promotion* if performance is minimally average or below the college's standard.

In fact, experts in personnel management cite perceived unfair treatment of employees as the leading cause of low morale. If affirmative action policies are applied fairly with integrity and discretion, they appear to help to overcome racism. However, if there is perceived unfairness, these policies seem to exacerbate and even enhance racism. These policies also pertain to other personnel actions, such as tenure, promotion, multiyear contracts, and early retirement benefits.

An institution's policies and practices related to admissions, retention, and graduation are also very significant, for these are areas that can be used to alleviate bigotry. It is important to encourage criteria that will retain high standards and quality while allowing all students equal opportunity, not only for admission but for retention up to graduation.

This approach is aided by the establishment of programs, such as tutorial and counseling centers, open to all students and reflecting diversity among the employees. Articulation agreements with high schools, two-year colleges, and graduate programs are a vital help to ensure that all students have evidence that they can begin and complete a full educational program. Curriculum should be reviewed by faculty for representative inclusiveness. A good curriculum should fairly and honestly include the contributions of all cultures and people. Most campuses have some measures whereby individuals who believe they have been treated unfairly have an opportunity for redress. Due process and appeal processes are important to allow all individuals to be heard in an impartial, unbiased forum of unquestioned integrity.

CHAPTER 4

"On the Outside Looking In"

MARIE McDEMMOND

I am an African American woman and former vice president of a large predominantly white southern university. The university is publicly supported and is one of the nine state universities in this state's system of higher education. It has over fifteen thousand students and a yearly annual operating budget of over $150 million, which supports five campuses of over one thousand acres and seventy-four buildings. The size of the budget, acreage, and buildings on the campuses are important to me, as I was the vice president for finance and chief operating officer of the university. I held that position for seven years, having served as the assistant vice president for one year before becoming vice president.

I have been in higher education administration and teaching for over twenty years. I hold a doctoral degree in higher education management from a large research university in the Northeast. My undergraduate work was done at a small black liberal arts college in the Deep South, and my master's degree was completed at a predominantly white state university, also in the Deep South. After teaching junior high school in my native city, I moved to the New York City area and began a ten-year stay in building a higher education career in New York State. During those ten years, I left higher education to gain practical financial management experience in hospital administration. After working in New York, I ventured farther north to a small northeastern state and initially was in charge of the finances for the state's community college system before taking a major financial position at the flagship campus of this state's university system. After four and a half years at the university and a traumatic experience, I left to become vice president and chief financial officer (CFO) at a small black college in a major Southeastern city. I later took an assistant vice president's position at a

71

predominantly white private major research university before leaving this particular city for personal reasons to return to my home state. After three years in my home state, during which time I was a full-time graduate faculty member at the predominantly white state university from which I received my master's degree, I moved to a different southern state to take a position at the university where I was formerly a vice president.

As a somewhat seasoned African American administrator on predominantly white campuses I have seen much change since the days of being called "black" and wearing Afros. As a woman whose area of responsibility was finance and management, which is still a white male bastion in American higher education, I have seen little change in this area. As a former chief financial officer now, I must be taken seriously and my positions and personal power carry weight within my institution. But even with my individual ascent, I am still an African American woman, and in the history of the life of these predominantly white institutions, little has changed since the influx of members of my race into these institutions in the late 1960s.

The Strength from Within

To share my experiences, I must start at the beginning of my career, to illustrate a very different career path than that followed by most others to the kind of top management position I hold. My background and training speak very much to who I am today. I was born in New Orleans, Louisiana, into an African American Catholic family. My parents graduated from Xavier University of Louisiana in the late 1920s. Like my parents before me, black Catholic education structured much of who I am today. As a little black girl in the South in the late 1950s and early 1960s, my career ambitions were developed by who and what I saw around me. So like my mother before me I wanted to become a teacher. By twenty-one years of age, I had accomplished that goal, and I spent two years teaching junior high students in a newly integrated (formerly white) junior high school in a disadvantaged area of New Orleans. Prior to that time, I had attended only black Catholic elementary and secondary institutions and the only black Catholic university in the United States, Xavier of Louisiana. My one experience in public education, prior to my first day on my new teaching job, had been my student teaching experience. I did my student teaching at an all black junior high school in a middle-class neighborhood in my home city. The fallacy of "separate but equal" echoed throughout my two years there, starting on the tour of the school that was given to new teachers.

Separate but equal—how often African Americans have heard those words. After spending four months student teaching in a one-building, poorly lighted, overcrowded black junior high, I entered a seven-building, freshly painted edifice that had been built for white junior high school students. The white students who attended this junior high were the children of blue-collar citizens of my home city—not at all like the students who attended the black junior high of my student teaching days where the students' parents were the black teachers, doctors, and business owners of the city. Whereas three hanging lights often provided the candle power for the middle-class black students, this white "equal" educational facility had three rows of fluorescent fixtures to assist in providing quality learning for the students. During my two years at the school, the number of white students declined as the number of black students increased.

From the first day in my profession, I knew I wanted to be the "boss" of the school. Immediately, I began to do what had worked for tens of thousands of African Americans—I went to school, this time to graduate school. Since by age twenty-one, I also had a husband and a newborn son, I continued to teach junior high while taking graduate courses in the evenings and summers. I applied to an institution within my home state's white higher education system and was immediately accepted to the master's program in educational administration, which was the training I believed I needed to become the boss of the school. For the first time, I entered the domain of white higher education and, as many African American students similarly experience today, I met immediate discrimination. On registration night I stood in line with fifty or more exhausted, but determined teachers. To my dismay, I was embarrassed by no one less than this university's dean of education. Being the aged southern gentleman that he was, he could not conceive why I had been accepted into the master's program in educational administration. As he fumbled and stuttered for a reason to deny me entrance, he glared at me. I naively began to explain my career aspirations to this man, who was the prototype of many more white male administrators I would encounter as my career took me to labor in the administration of higher education.

After a conversation that was far too loud for a dean and graduate student to be engaged in while standing in a registration line, I was forced to declare secondary education as my major. The dean finally concluded that since he could not openly use race and sex as reasons for denying me registration in the educational administration major, my age would be the factor. With the same determination that I would use to minimize future obstacles throughout my professional career in higher education management, I conceded to his declaration of my major as secondary education, but I enrolled in the hardest courses that were available in educational statistics and foundations. At the same time, I began to plan the next steps I would take to facilitate my becoming an administrator. I was not about to let some elderly white conservative dictate my future career due to his preconceived notions of who should be an educational administrator. With twelve hours of straight

A coursework under my belt, I again petitioned the dean's office for admission into the educational administration program.

To enhance my chances, I had chosen as my advisor and chair of my thesis committee the most respected senior member of the college's graduate faculty. This faculty member provided credibility to my reapplication and spoke on my behalf, and by my third semester, I was formally admitted. I received a master's in education administration in 1972 and was later to find out that I was the only African American to that date to receive a master's in this discipline from this particular institution. Although I achieved my goal, I had to take a required course from the dean. Although I waited until my last semester to do so, I received from him my only B in my master's program. From this experience, I learned that everyone has his or her way to get even. Learning this lesson early in my professional career has provided me, I believe, with a sixth sense in being more circumspect in my administrative functioning. I never make a decision or influence an individual without thinking what that person's opposite viewpoint will be or how he or she will react to my position. Being prepared for the "getting even" has added a little longevity to my survival and sanity to my experiences in predominantly white colleges and universities.

Getting to the Inside

My career in higher education began in 1970 when I moved with my first husband to Westchester County, New York, so he could take a position with a major Fortune 500 Corporation. Anxious about obtaining certification to teach junior high in New York State (I later received permanent certification from kindergarten through twelfth grade), I sorted out other career paths while my certification was being processed. My exploration led me to a small private college in southern Westchester County that had just begun a program to meet one of its new missions—the education of minority (mainly black and Hispanic) students. I became this college's first director of its still existing minority student program. Much discussion is held today about minority student programs and affirmative action being dead end career paths for minority administrators in predominantly white colleges and universities. Indeed, for several of my colleagues who began with me in these programs in the early 1970s, this limitation has been true. However, many others have branched out and hold other administrative positions, mainly in the area of student affairs.

My experiences as a minority student program director taught me the foundations of every aspect of higher education. Unlike many positions in institutions that are limited to work in the financial, academic, or student affairs areas, those who administer minority student programs touch all aspects of the student and institutional lives. I had to learn about things in several different areas from academic requirements to student financial aid to dormitory management, all the way to university relations and development, as funding for students was a priority. With an active community advisory board and students who often got involved in negative town/gown encounters, my skills as an arbitrator and university relations "spinner" were developed. Managing money from all fund sources (institutional, federal, state, and private) increased my knowledge of different budgetary, accounting, and auditing requirements. Again with my ambition to be the "boss," I learned quickly that the control of funds was very important to leadership and being the boss in higher education. I saw the college's treasurer limit or scuttle many programs with the simple statement, "There is no money in the budget for that." To me the lesson became very simple. If I wanted my programs and students to succeed, I had to know about, and control, the financial resources. By demonstrating to university administrators the financial viability of minority student programs, I was able to put the program more into the mainstream and to make it more of an essential part of this small private college's financial picture, if not the total college life.

Life on the Inside

Outspokenness has added (or subtracted) to my climb in higher education management. As I reflect on my professional career, there was one traumatic experience of my outspokenness that changed the course of my development and, indeed if the outcome had been different, might have destroyed me and my professional career forever. In the early 1980s I spent four and one-half years at a major research university in the Northeast. As a state institution, this campus is the flagship of its system and has been considered to be a "minority sensitive" campus, having had an African American as its chief executive officer (CEO) prior to my employment there. I was hired in the early 1980s as the budget director, the second African American, but the first woman to hold that position. I was appointed after a grueling three-day interview process by a relatively new CEO, who after several months began to utilize my management abilities in other areas. He gave me increased responsibilities and a change of title to assistant chancellor within a year. After two years he left to become CEO of a larger research university in the western part of the United States, and the provost was appointed acting CEO. The provost and I previously had not seen eye to eye on many critical funding issues, and in fact, we competed with each other to determine who could exert more influence on the CEO. More than anything, this provost desired to become the permanent CEO. He had not been selected for the number one slot when he was acting CEO at another university. His aspiration was still to become a CEO, even though some people admonished his curt management style.

During the period that he was acting chancellor, which was somewhat protracted due to search processes in higher education, he appointed an Asian person to a position as assistant chancellor and limited my scope of responsibilities as assistant chancellor. Ultimately, the provost's expectations of becoming permanent CEO were not realized and a new CEO, who was external to the campus, was selected. This new CEO had not held an administrative position in a major institution of higher education and, while having political experience, was somewhat unprepared for the viciousness and sub rosa nature of academic politics. He immediately wanted to reorganize the administration and place my functions under the vice president for administration and finance, a man who went to undergraduate school at this particular institution and worked his way up from a position of assistant personnel coordinator. The vice president had never worked at another institution, nor had he pursued his education beyond his bachelor's degree.

While on the surface it may have appeared that the circumstances I have described were due to the arrival of a new CEO who wanted to reorganize and form his own team, one needs to look below the surface to find what I believed was the true reason for the changes. One had to look at the history of my involvement on this campus as a backdrop to this situation. From my first day, I had become very involved in African American and women's issues, not only at this institution, but statewide. My outspokenness and belief that groups can influence and cause change to happen more than individuals can do so led me to reactivate the campus' withered minority professional organization. I became president of a regional (eight-state) minority women's group, and I became active in a statewide group of minority educators in higher education, eventually becoming its president for two years. In addition, I became involved in improving minority students' performance on campus and securing the financial aid needed for them to succeed.

I prepared legislative testimony on the impact of financial aid to student success and presented it to legislators in conjunction with the Hispanic director of financial aid, who was later to leave for a higher position in a western state. When he left the university, I was appointed as a member of the search committee for the new director of financial aid. After a long, open search, I used my powers of persuasion on the committee to influence the appointment of the African American who held the position of associate director to the director's spot. In my estimation, he was as qualified as if not more so than any of the external candidates interviewed (none of whom had been a minority). The committee knew that the appointing authority (who was the recently appointed Asian assistant chancellor) did not want this man selected. After much stalling, high-level foot dragging, and internal dissent, the African American male whom I endorsed was appointed to the director's position. I saw this process as one in which I had to be engaged, not only because the African American man was the most qualified, but also because he could make certain that minority students received their fair share of the financial aid allocations, which is the key to these students' retention and graduation.

Following this bloodless battle, I was called in by the vice chancellor who had appointed me to the search committee. He wanted to discuss with me my role in the search process. He made it clear to me, as did my boss, the CEO who appointed me, and other officers of the university, that I should not have gotten involved so adamantly in supporting a particular candidate. Since the two men believed that my motives were only racially motivated, they admonished me, saying that my actions should be dictated first and foremost by my role as a university administrator. After much discussion on this point, I finally presented my position—I had to let them know that I responded and made decisions because of who I was and what I believed to be right, and those realities started with my being an African American woman. This declaration concerned many of those around me, and I became ostracized from the "inner circle" where my input previously had been valued. This event laid the foundation upon which an openly aired discrimination case would later be built. In higher education, individual personalities and ambitions can influence greatly the course of events. While I cannot second guess the motives of any individual, I can present situations that existed. When the newly appointed CEO arrived on campus and wanted to reorganize, I could not see it as a benign series of events, but rather as a contrived arrangement by some people to further diminish my influence in the decision-making processes of the university.

When he arrived, the new CEO wanted narrative descriptions of each of his major areas and resumes of administrators that directly reported to him. From the date of his selection, all communications were filtered through my peer, the new assistant chancellor. No one could communicate with the CEO without her screening the data or interpreting the material. While I probably should have been more concerned about this situation, I felt that once he started, my communications with him would be direct and he would understand my value to the university. But that did not happen, and he began to reorganize.

My reaction to his plan was immediate and direct. I met with the new CEO and informed him that I believed the reorganization, so soon after his coming and before meeting with me, was not in his or the university's best interest. I tried to explain to him that the state and university's budgeting processes were fairly complex and that he should make time available for me to explain these and my other responsibilities to him in detail before making his decision to reorganize. I stressed this situation particularly since the vice chancellor for administration and finance had not been involved in any university-wide budgeting issues. The new CEO did not accept my rationale, and his only responses centered on his not wanting too many persons reporting directly to him. I even suggested that I report directly to him for an interim period until he learned the key financial/budgetary impacts of my position, after which I would report to the vice chancellor. Nothing I could present or say, when he would give me a brief time to do so, made any difference. His mind was made up.

I then had to reconsider all the circumstances of the last year, especially the CEO's gracious offer to make me an associate vice chancellor, with a five thousand dollar salary raise and a five-year contract (which was in violation of university personnel policies). Even with the attractive aspects of this offer, I felt I was being removed from my assistant chancellorship and the direct reporting line to the CEO because of who I was and the positions that I had taken. While I felt I had been taken seriously in my position prior to this time, I now felt many people had done so by not seeing or recognizing my blackness. I was most often described as a woman, rather than as a black or African American administrator. Many people wanted to perceive me only as a woman administrator, who just happened to be black. I did not just happen to be black, and when I made them aware of this reality, complications occurred. I then knew what was happening to me. It appeared that this new CEO had been "warned" against my becoming too close to his administration and the way my decisions and advice to him would be perceived by others on campus. This new organizational structure would alleviate any future problems in this area. I knew then that I had no other course; I had to tell the new CEO that I felt his reorganization was discriminatory to me as a black woman and was retaliation for positions I had taken in support of other blacks on campus. I told him I would file a discrimination case against him and the university.

One must always be ready when one takes a strong position. I did not do so without preparing myself, my family, and my staff. I had already gone through the personal guilt that one has when you feel there must be some other reason for a person's actions besides discrimination. I had questioned over and over on many sleepless nights and long telephone conversations with trusted friends far away, "What had I done?" "Hadn't I faithfully fulfilled all my duties, even driving to the state capitol in a blinding snow storm at seven months pregnant?" "Hadn't I been committed to this university?" "Wasn't I a good manager?" "Didn't I know my area, and hadn't I performed my duties in an outstanding manner?" I soon realized that I could not let self-doubt destroy me; I could not let others' fear of me or their own personal ambitions stand in the way of my professional career. My path became crystallized.

I selected an attorney who had been involved in other discrimination cases both in the town and in the state capital. He was from another ethnic group and was well respected. He was not afraid that the university would blackball him within the local legal community, an important fact in small college towns. I told him the story and found myself in disbelief as I do now and as I have each time I have reflected on it since then. After several weeks and with this attorney's assistance the university realized it had violated its own personnel policies. More important, however, the university acknowledged that it would not be in its own best interest to have me file a discrimination complaint. An amicable settlement was reached, and after two years I took a position as chief financial officer at another smaller institution.

When I achieved the level of vice president of administration and fiinance at a large predominantly white university, I found some things changed. I was appointed by a CEO who is committed to expand educational and professional opportunities for women and African Americans. Out of five vice presidents there was another woman (white) vice president and another African American (male) vice president. There were at least five deans (out of nine) who were women, and one who was an African American woman. These statistics were better than those of most colleges and universities in the country. In fact, women and minorities held more top administrative positions at my former university than any other in that southern state's university system. Even with this progress, there are situations that I encountered as the highest ranking African American woman administrator at the university that shows little has changed. Let me describe one problematic series of events.

During one year, I was contacted individually by three African American women administrators. One I knew well; one I had only met briefly; the other I had not known until she walked into my office. All three of these women independently came to me to discuss what they felt had been discrimination in either the denial of a promotion or in performing their duties. Two of the three women had been at the university for over five years. All three voiced their concerns over one high-level white male administrator's actions. As an officer of the university, I felt I had to inform the CEO. He immediately asked the university's affirmative action officer and the university ombudsman to investigate these complaints. After a two-month review, which included interviews of many university personnel, a report was issued to the CEO. Although this report was submitted in confidence, the white male administrator was outraged. He went to an external attorney and claimed, in his own exhaustive report, that I, for motives he hypothesized were resource allocation based, instigated these charges against him. As are many African Americans in predominantly white colleges and universities, I was called upon by those like me to hear their concerns and to assist them when they felt no one else would. For taking action well within the scope of my position as a officer of the university, I was accused of siding with those of my race and sex for some other reasons. Again, I found that I had to defend myself and my actions for no other reason than that I was a female African American administrator on a predominantly white campus. Again I questioned myself, "What had I done wrong?" "Had I overstepped my boundaries as a university

administrator," and, if I had, "why?" This time I resorted to the "weapon" of
my "attacker." I wrote a well-structured response to the CEO, explaining my
actions and reasons for them. The situation finally died down; for other reasons the white male administrator was removed.

The Future Inside

What will the future hold for me and others like me on predominantly
white campuses? Demographics predict that the number of minority students
in the population will increase. Will the numbers of African American administrators and faculty increase as well? I have serious doubts that they will.

As more and more African American students enter our institutions, there
is less of a focus on affirmative action. Sure, there are all the same number
of reports to fill out, the same number of places to announce job vacancies,
and the same lip service paid to "finding" qualified minorities for positions.
However, in the institutions I have observed, numbers have decreased as
some African American administrators move on or are forced out. In more
cases than not, African American administrators are replaced by a member of
the majority. As long as all the t's were crossed, i's were dotted, and the right
affirmative action reports filled out, these predominantly white institutions
feel they have done their jobs, even though our numbers do not increase.

We as African Americans must take it upon ourselves to help each other
achieve and to increase our numbers. We must be willing to go the extra mile
and assist other minorities in obtaining, retaining, and advancing in administrative positions in higher education. There are ways in which we can accomplish this. We must serve as mentors and sounding boards for younger
African American administrators and faculty members. For me, one way to
accomplish this is my own personal mentoring efforts. I have conducted a
summer mentoring program for African American females at my institution
who are interested in increasing their knowledge of financial management.
One African American female administrator from the student affairs area who
worked with me four summers ago is now an assistant vice president in my
area of responsibility on one of the campuses in our system. Another effort
we started at my former institution will increase knowledge held by women
and minorities of the decision-making processes of the institution and assist
them in advancing. Each year we selected four to six middle-level managers
who are interested in upward mobility. They worked with selected upper-
level administrators on tasks and projects during the year. From this number,
two persons were selected to participate in national training programs in
higher education administration. Upon successful completion of these two
programs, the individuals were appointed to positions at the director level or
above in the institution. The advantages of a program like this one is that the

minorities and women selected are provided with a career ladder within the institution. They also will serve as role models for other younger or less experienced staff. Regardless of the particular program that may be structured, it is incumbent upon African Americans to face the reality that we must come together and help each other if we are to succeed in the future in predominantly white institutions of higher education.

Another mechanism of support is often found in campus-based African American and/or minority staff and faculty organizations. Most campuses have had such groups for years, if African Americans exist in any appreciable numbers on campuses. Some state systems also may have statewide organizations, similar to the one of which I was president in a state in the Northeast.

As an African American woman and one who is active in women's groups, I have been able to observe how support groups of women and support groups of African Americans and/or minorities are treated differently on campuses. From my observations, women's groups are better structured and better received on these predominantly white campuses than are African American and/or minority groups. African American and/or minority groups do not appear to garner as much support from their members, who often appear less interested and less committed to the organization than do women's groups.

In addition to the African American administrators and faculty on campuses, our paramount concern must be for African American students, for it is the student that education is about. How are African American students doing on predominantly white campuses? To answer this we must look at some of the external trends. College tuitions are increasing, within both public and private institutions, at a rate of over 6 percent per year. Most predominantly white private colleges are already out of the price range of most African American students, even those who receive maximum financial aid. Large loans must be taken, and if the student is not successful in completing his or her degree, he or she leaves the institution with a large indebtedness and without any available means to repay. Public institutions, in order to cope with high applicant demand, and maybe even to be more elite, are raising admissions standards, which cuts out a larger and larger portion of African American students as SAT admissions requirements increase.

As I focus on the future, however, I must be somewhat optimistic. There will remain the "token" ones of us who have made it to the policy-making positions on these predominantly white campuses. If we understand the issues, we must continue to be the conscience of these institutions and mandate that they respond to our needs and those of our students. All of us must pledge ourselves to this unending mission.

CHAPTER 5

"A Meaningful Contribution"

HORACE JUDSON

I believe that many African American higher education administrators often have common academic preparation experiences. Many of us graduated from and served for several years as a member of the faculty and administration of a historically black college or university (HBCU). I served for seventeen years as a faculty member and administrator at Morgan State University, including five years as the vice president of academic affairs.

The Decision and the Search

Around 1985, after serving four years as chairman of the Chemistry Department at Morgan State, I began to consider very seriously whether I wanted to complete my academic career at one institution. For the first time, I considered predominantly white institutions as an option, though at first I was reluctant and uncomfortable with such a notion. In 1968, after having accepted a position as a senior research chemist at a major petrochemical corporation, I had changed my career plans because of my undeniable, deeply felt commitment to advancing HBCUs in general, and to increasing the number of black physical scientists in particular. At the completion of my doctorate, ten interview trips to major corporations resulted in nine job offers, including several almost desperate recruitment efforts, and left me indelibly impressed with the tragedy of the paucity of black physical scientists. But over time a growing concern within the black community about the welfare of the 80 percent of black students who were enrolled at predominantly white institutions, a strong confidence that I could make a meaningful contribution, and a long-term curiosity about working in the "other" institutions persuaded me to explore the possibilities.

My job searches among predominantly white institutions resulted in four finalist interviews in three western states and one New England state. I accepted three of the offers for on-campus interviews, declining the one at a downtown campus of a large urban university. This process was a new experience for me, since my earlier venture into administration at Morgan State resulted from an internal search and was essentially a direct presidential appointment. The three positions for which I interviewed were all different: a deanship of a College of Arts, Letters, and Sciences; a vice presidency for academic and student affairs; and an assistant vice presidency for academic affairs and research in the central administration of a system. The three interviews resulted in two job offers, the deanship and the system assistant vice presidency, one in California; and the other in New England. Certainly having both searches result in offers was a positive experience, and the interviews themselves were rather uneventful. The California search committee seemed not to have had knowledge of my race prior to my visit, as confirmed by comments of members of the search committee as well as by African American staff and faculty. The New England committee had known about my race and ethnicity because the president personally knew one of my references.

The third interview—the one which did not result in an offer—was an unpleasant surprise. A couple of aspects of this situation bordered on the crass. The institution was located in a small town in an isolated area of the state. Even though there were few blacks in the area, there were significant percentages of Hispanics and native Americans. I did not see a single black faculty member or student, although I remembered being told that there were a few black students. I saw one black staff person, although there may have been a few others at the institution.

The campus was approximately a one-and-one-half-hour drive from the airport. The person who met me there and drove me to the campus was a black secretary, the only black staff person I met or saw while there. The president was an impressive, friendly person who spoke believably about his commitment to diversity. The second and final day of the visit included a session with the Faculty Senate, which was open to all faculty. I was introduced, and the floor was opened for questions. After several long minutes of silence, which seemed an eternity for me, I realized that not one of the more than forty faculty members present was going to ask a question. After surveying the many embarrassed faces, I finally broke the silence by declaring with a forced smile that I would avail myself of the opportunity to ask them questions, if they had none for me. I knew then I would not accept an offer if one were made. I wondered at the time, and still do, what their behavior meant. Was it planned? Were they dumbfounded by the possibility of having an African American vice president? Why was the faculty's behavior a polar opposite to the president's?

Even though I had spent essentially my whole academic career at a predominantly black university up to 1986, I had no significant concerns about switching to a predominantly white institution. My five years in graduate school convinced me that not only could I survive in an atmosphere where there were few blacks, but that I could form strong positive social and academic relationships in such an environment. Moreover, I could deal effectively with instances of overt and subtle racism, of which I experienced many during that period. Racism at elite, prestigious academic institutions, perpetrated by the distinguished and the aspiring-to-be distinguished, is often harder to fathom because it is naively unexpected. It was during my graduate school days that I adopted an approach to questionable, hostile, and insulting acts or behavior directed at me. I at first presume that such acts or behavior have an explanation other than racism, and only if no other plausible explanation can be found do I consider racism. I found that I could resolve most problematic situations effectively, even forcefully, without getting bogged down in charges of racism and the nonproductive counter-reactions. I still find such an approach successful, and moreover such an approach deals effectively with the racists without unfairly charging others whose unpleasantness is not generated by racism. The latter includes most of us. Of course I respond to overt racism directly and immediately as befits the act.

I accepted the deanship of the College of Arts, Letters, and Sciences at a relatively small university (five thousand students at that time) in a very large system. The college contained over 70 percent of the total students, credit hours, faculty, and departments in the university. It is located in a major agricultural belt, an area undergoing a significant transition due to businesses transferring in and rapidly developing bedroom communities. It is one of the state's fastest growing regions. It also was, and still is, a very conservative region where not too many years ago crosses were burned in a community a few miles north of the campus. It is a relatively young campus, just over thirty years old. When I arrived, many of the faculty had spent their entire careers here, having little direct experiences with other institutions. The typical student was a thirty-year-old female commuter. There were four African American faculty and four Hispanic faculty out of two hundred; there were a couple of dozen black and Hispanic staff. The staff occupied mostly clerical positions and positions in plant operations and grounds.

During my interview trip I was met at the airport by a member of the search committee. The two-day visit was interesting, very pleasant, and tiring. Each day was tightly scheduled, with very little free time. The social affair during the evening of the first day was warm, friendly, and enjoyable. I felt very welcomed. The various constituents seemed pleased, some even excited about my candidacy. Questions posed at the different sessions were thoughtful and appropriate; some were posed to test my abilities; others were posed to learn of my experiences; still others out of seemingly genuine curiosity about me at a personal level. The president impressed me as a person strongly and seriously committed to diversity in all of its aspects. He expressed the desire to provide strong academic leadership for the university's largest and most important college. He confided in me that several of the campus' most influential faculty had been very impressed by my qualifications, experiences, and interpersonal skills. I found out later that one senior faculty member, who was distrustful and critical of affirmative action programs, had remarked that I was clearly the best candidate and that affirmative action was not a consideration. One harbinger of things to come was the indication by a senior administrator of a brown/black problem on campus. He warned that Hispanics were upset with the success of blacks relative to that of Hispanics. Overall, the visit was a tremendously positive experience. The campus was beautiful; the academic community was hospitable. I was enthusiastic to start.

The Beginning/Institutional Differences and Similarities

After accepting the deanship, I was extremely busy the first few months undergoing the orientation and adjustment of a newcomer. In many ways, perhaps most, I found academic administration on a predominantly white campus very much the same as that on a predominantly black campus, as I had presumed. There were important differences, however; some manifested themselves immediately, others over time.

This campus recently had achieved university status and was still undergoing the transition from a "college to a university." Much of the previous focus had been on adding programs and departments to achieve the minimum number of degree programs and departments required by the system. When I arrived, a great deal of attention was directed toward organizational structures and faculty-administration relationships. There was still much talk about the period prior to the incumbent president when the relationship between faculty and administrators was abysmal and hostile. There were many "war" stories of faculty being abused and administrators run out of office. I was warned of the "end-runs" that faculty made in order to bypass the dean for direct access to the vice president and president, or to bypass the vice president for direct access to the president. The president wanted administrative leadership from me, and the faculty wanted academic leadership of and for the faculty of the college. The faculty-administrative tension was not unlike my previous experience and probably not atypical of most institutions of higher education, except there seemed to be a deeper than normal distrust of administrators by the faculty here. There seemed to be less collegiality among the faculty, not the same closeness that I believe existed at my previous campus. I wondered initially if this was a factor of unionization or maybe my inability as a minority administrator to observe or to experience accurately the faculty-faculty relationships. My present perception is that there was less collegiality at this institution than there was at another university where I previously worked.

There also seemed to be more concern about administrative matters and less about academic matters. Again, part of the explanation could be the existence of collective bargaining. Nevertheless, I was disquieted by what seemed to me a greater interest by many faculty and by the faculty leadership in the appointment and termination of administrators than in curriculum review and reform, and in academic program evaluation; more interest in the furniture purchased by a vice president than in establishing a functional peer review system. In short, the faculty seemed to take less ownership of and express fewer concerns about academic matters, matters which I consider as predominantly under the purview of the faculty. Some of the differences I perceived were probably differences between a young, twenty-six-year-old institution with few, if any, traditions and not well articulated institutional voices, and a much older, 120-year-old institution with long-established, proven values. They also may have been the differences between an institution of a large system and one with an independent board. At the historically black university I left and the one at which I matriculated, faculty and administrators felt their culture, history, and future were inextricably interwoven with the university and the welfare of its students; they viewed the university as an institution essential to the survival and advancement of the community. In my opinion, such was not the case at my most recent institution. This university was one where, in the most admirable and positive way, faculty and administrators practice their professions and staff perform their duties. Even though most individuals are very dedicated and industrious, their links to the university are more as a valued place of employment than as a foundation of their community, a repository of their cultural heritage and an essentiality for their children's future.

Of course, there is the understandable and expected difference between an academic environment where most faculty, staff, and students look like you and one where most do not. In addition, the community external to the university, with an African American population under 3 percent, accentuated the contrast for me and my family. Even though this was not a significant concern, it nevertheless provided a total environment that was understandably not quite as warm, inviting, and supportive, although it was hospitable, respectful, and correct.

When I arrived at my new institution, the black faculty at first seemed distant and not as engaging as I had expected. All four had tenure, and three were full professors. Maybe they were not quite sure how they should relate to me or appear to relate. They were far less assertive in getting acquainted with me and making social contact and inviting me to social activities than were their nonblack counterparts. Maybe they felt that politically this was in my own best interest. The African American staff was different; just the opposite, in fact. They introduced themselves, availed themselves of every opportunity to talk, and offered to help in any way possible. They also provided me with an introduction to the African American community, as well as the white community and other minority communities. The staff was also not shy about sharing their problems with me, mostly problems related to racism. They had not been promoted, given credit for their accomplishments, provided with professional development opportunities, or given equitable work loads, and so on. Several nonblack faculty also were assertive in getting acquainted and in inviting me to social affairs and offering to help me in any way possible. Several wrote me before my arrival, congratulating me and pledging support. One person expressed how much he was impressed with my experience and qualifications.

My initial experiences with African American students here were dissimilar to the experiences of my previous eighteen years with African American students. It was difficult for me to engage them in a conversation of any length. Some seemed surprised at my presence and very reticent to converse. My inquiries about their interests, concerns, and aspirations solicited very few responses. Since there were only about 150 blacks enrolled, I was surprised at how few knew each other. There was a Black Student Union, but few students participated in it, and at least two expressed hostility toward it. I was struck that most students spoke to me with their eyes and head diverted downward, almost never looking me in the eyes. Just recently an African American administrative colleague at a nearby institution related similar experiences with African American students there. Invitations to my office for informal chats were rarely accepted. There were noticeable changes over a five year period, however. The BSU, UMOJA, has grown and has become very active. I found the rate of low participation of African American students in nonathletic university organizations and various activities to be very troublesome. Further, other staff and I had very little success in increasing their participation. I was unable to accept my ineffectual relationship and the ineffectual relationships of the other African American faculty and staff with African American students. This situation is foreign to me. One of the most fulfilling aspects of my academic career, both as a faculty member and an administrator, was my close relationship with the students, a relationship akin to one found in a close-knit family. That relationship did not exist in this particular setting generally for students, whites, or minorities. And according to my colleagues and my own observations, such a relationship does not exist at most institutions.

The surrounding Hispanic and black communities viewed this university as irrelevant to their concerns at best and racist at worst. The poor relations with the minority communities had been established from the university's founding to the time of my president's predecessor. The Hispanic and black communities felt that the university was hostile to them and their students. The president was deeply committed to addressing these concerns of the minority community and to transforming the university into a diverse, multicultural academic community. Some people, especially some faculty, felt the president was obsessed with diversity and affirmative action, and, consequently, he had several highly vocal opponents. The issue of affirmative action was a hot one at the outset of my tenure and continued to be a significant concern.

Expectations of Me

From the start of my deanship, through my tenure as provost/vice president for academic affairs I enjoyed strong overall support from the faculty, staff, and fellow administrators. Based on feedback from visitations for university accreditation and special program accreditations, as well as from an evaluation team for the president, I am viewed by many, maybe even most, of the faculty as an effective administrator and a strong academic leader. I was identified as having earned trust and respect and as a person with a vision for the university. I am confident that I had strong supporters among all of the constituent groups. However, my tenure there was anything but a bed of roses. That probably would be the case for any university administrator of any race or ethnicity. There was, however, an added dimension of difficulty and complexity for a minority administrator. The issue of race is never far away, and it manifests itself in many ways. This is true even for those of us who ascribe racism to a given situation or incident only as a last resort. There were many significant expectations relative to diversity and affirmative action, some distinctly articulated and others implied. These came from various sources; higher level administrators, African American staff, African American faculty, the African American community, African American students, other faculty, staff, and administrative colleagues.

There was a clear charge for me to be a signal player in achieving the university's, or at least the president's, diversity and affirmative action goals and an expectation by the president as well as the African American staff that I would make linkages with the African American community and increase the presence and participation of that community within the university, as well as increase the number of African American students. Of course I was expected to increase the number of all underrepresented students, as well as to increase the overall student population. Early on, I made contact with the African American community and hosted several functions on campus for them. Not surprisingly, they requested my participation in various community projects of various types: educational, political, and social. Some people at the university and some in the community unrealistically expected immediate significant results from those increased interactions.

In the main, the faculty's opinions relative to me were unrelated to my race. They wanted me to be a strong, effective academic leader, a first among equals. Still externally imposed and/or self-imposed responsibilities related to race pose formidable additional challenges, if not burdens. Some African American community members expected me to be able to provide university financial support for community projects, or to provide facilities on short notice and without cost. Some white faculty thought I would have a magical answer for their relationship problems with an African American student or staff member. These situations did not occur from malevolent intentions or some diabolical plot; intentions were mostly honest and often even admirable. Even though I was cognizant of the danger of overextending myself or expending too much energy because of the never-ending requests made to minorities due to our rarity, it was difficult to avoid the trap.

Because I was an African American, or an administrator, and particularly because I was an African American administrator, the invitations, requests, and appointments were abundant: standing committees, search committees, ad hoc committees, task forces, boards, speeches, panels, adjudications—and so on. These solicitations came from inside the university and outside, from schools, civic groups, social groups, political groups, charitable groups, and learned societies. Many requests came clearly because of my administrative position, but many just as clearly were connected to race. How could I preach diversity and multiculturalism and deny the requesters the diversity that my views and presence would bring, when often there were very few alternative potential participants available? Moreover, I wanted to participate maximally.

I wanted to inform, educate, enlighten, and learn by engaging in every dialogue possible. I perceived a great opportunity in this environment, which was undergoing rapid transition. Even though thoroughly aware of the danger of stretching myself too thin, it was difficult to say no. Commitments coming one by one seemed manageable, but they soon became serious consumers of my time. These worthwhile but time-consuming activities were not viewed as a significant part of my primary role and responsibilities. And even though the president voiced strong encouragement and approval for my diversity activities, he certainly expected me to perform my primary duties at a level, qualitatively and quantitatively, equal to or exceeding the levels of my white administrative colleagues. In short, all of these important, serious, and time-consuming commitments related to diversity and multiculturalism were in addition to "regular" duties and responsibilities. They were overloads. The irony is that at every opportunity I warn new minority faculty, staff, and administrators to avoid this irresistible bog. I urge faculty in particular to focus their energy and time on those efforts leading to the achievement of promotion and tenure, especially scholarship. If faculty colleagues or administrators encourage participation on committees or in community activities, the minority faculty or administrator should request a clear and definitive relationship between promotion, tenure, and performance evaluation and those activities.

I mentored minority faculty, students, and administrators (and some nonminority also). I invested a large amount of time in community activities, especially those related to the university community. I participated in a number of efforts to increase the success rates of minority students in K through twelve and college. It was a conscious choice, a labor of love. I still do it because I can do it, and I still survive and succeed in my profession. Having had significant prior administrative experience was critical to my ability to maintain successfully this difficult balancing act. I doubt if I could have survived had this been my first major administrative post. The stress, the uncertainties, and the unknowns may have undone a neophyte.

As I mentioned previously, the search activities involving predominantly white universities were the first regular academic search processes in which I participated. My entry into administration in 1973 resulted from a direct appeal by the president of the university. I was a young faculty member and had never thought about becoming an administrator, and I did not find the notion appealing. I was almost shocked by the offer of an associate deanship and was very hesitant to accept. I accepted on condition that I could teach half-time. The president had become aware of me through my participation on the Board for Salary, Promotion, and Tenure; my chairmanship of the Student Services Task Force; my advisorship to undergraduate student researchers in chemistry; and my outspokenness at faculty meetings and in the campus community. One year after my appointment to the associate deanship of the college, the vice president for academic affairs resigned, and I was offered that position. Extensive consultation took place with the faculty and students, and the appointment was made without a formal search. I was vice president for academic affairs at that HBCU for five years, having served two presidents. I believe that the president who appointed me would have been an effective mentor to me, since he had indicated such a commitment, but he had left for another position before I assumed office. The president under whom I served the longest, for four years, did not establish a mentor relationship with me. At the time of my appointment to the vice presidency, I was a young, thirty-three year-old administrator with very little experience. I earned my experience the hard way, without the benefit of a mentor. Too often I was brash, impatient, and undiplomatic. Some said that my energy and goal attainments compensated for my deficits while I underwent administrative maturation.

There were few surprises and no significant difficulties with respect to performing my administrative duties and establishing myself as an academic leader in my present institution. The issues, concerns, and complaints were similar to those of my previous administrative tenure. For the most part, I could have closed my eyes and not have perceived any differences from the previous university. In other words, essentially, faculty is faculty, staff is staff, students are students, administrators are administrators, irrespective of demographics. I was the dean, not the black dean. And I felt, acted, and in the main was treated that way. Even though my experience there was mostly unrelated to race, the few times when race was an issue were distracting and painful and sometimes exhausting. It is easy to see how such times could potentially discourage and even derail a minority administrator.

The Large University System

The bureaucracy associated with an extraordinarily large system was different for me and often frustrating, stultifying, and demotivating. Budget allocations were never complete. They oozed from one year to the next, and the figures continually changed. It was difficult to accept such a reality. I am not sure I ever really did. I had worried that moving from a nonunion campus to a unionized system would be problematic, but here my worry was unfounded. In spite of philosophical differences with some of the unions' positions, I found working with the union leadership and within the framework of collective bargaining to have been an unexpected positive experience. Faculty union leadership on the campus offered our working relationship and effective communications as a model for the system. I think the collective bargaining agreements and effective union representatives may actually minimize acts of racism. At least on this particular campus, minorities in collective bargaining units trusted their representatives and the system to address grievances, often at the informal level, which might otherwise have developed into issues of racism.

One great advantage of being in a large system was the opportunity to network with the many system colleagues. I formed many professional relationships as a dean and a vice president. The opportunities to share information and discuss mutual problems and explore solutions were enormously important. The ability to speak on an ongoing basis with a dozen or so colleagues who are familiar with your situation would probably not exist as readily without the system. I grew professionally from these contacts and formed very good friendships. We networked not only systemwide, but within groups within the system, an African American network and a minorities network. It is important for minorities to network for information and provide mutual support. It is just as important, maybe more so, to network outside of your own racial or ethnic group. Otherwise, you will limit your own growth and development, your access to information, and you will miss out on getting to know some terrific people. While it is important for a minority group to share knowledge within the group, failure to reach beyond the group limits the total group knowledge as well as that of each individual member. As one friend put it, "I want to know what we know, but I also want to know what they know." I think it is also important to help them understand what we know and what we feel and why. In addition, my system colleagues provided external points of reference against which I can normalize my own views, perceptions, and actions.

Diversity: Good Intentions; Unintended Consequences

Many of the actions taken by the administrative leadership in a predominantly white institution to increase diversity raise the issue of equity. Though well-intentioned, a questionable action often increases cynicism and frustration of supporters and nonsupporters. For example, the president, through administrative reorganization and position reclassification, provided upward mobility to several minorities. This decision was made in the academic year prior to my joining the university, but the effective date coincided with my appointment, in 1986. Two African Americans and one Hispanic were "promoted." The positions provided more visibility for the minorities as well as increased responsibilities. Prior to the elevation, the administration included no Hispanics or African Americans and the highest level of these appointments held were assistant vice president, director, and associate director. Very soon after my arrival, I became aware of the simmering controversy. Some people complained about the highest degrees held by the appointees, especially concerning two of these appointees; one had a master's degree, the other a bachelor's. The third individual also had a master's, but this appointment was not an issue.

Some complaints were raised about the noncompetitive method of the appointments, and some regarded one of the appointments in particular as favoritism, viewing it as an effort to remove an individual from a previous position of risk. Several faculty and administrators felt no reluctance to speak critically, even derisively, in my presence or directly to me about one or more of these appointments. One outspoken faculty member saw it as plain evidence of the president's misguided, obsessive commitment to affirmative action. Being new to the campus and mindful of my strong disposition to respond unequivocally to such provocation, I decided it was best to exercise restraint and discretion. Finally one day, after enduring a few months of sporadic lamentations, I had had enough.

On an occasion when a department chairperson, who had been and remained one of my strongest supporters, expressed disbelief that the assistant vice president could occupy such a position at such a high salary level without a doctorate, in a calm voice, but loud enough for the other chairpersons present to hear, I expressed my inability to understand her concern. I went on to point out that a white male, who was also in student services, occupied a similar administrative position, but with far fewer duties and responsibilities, yet made a higher salary even though he did not have a master's degree. After a noticeable silence, she responded that she had been unaware that the other administrator possessed only a bachelor's degree. To which I continued, "But you surely knew he did not have a doctorate." After that, I heard of no similar negative comments about the appointments. It is unlikely that any feelings had changed. A year later, there was a clear consensus that two of the appointees had served competently in their roles, particularly one of them. The third had been reassigned by his supervisor within the first year and soon was out of administration. Those appointments, which the president felt were a necessary first step to achieving the university's diversity goals, as well as a strong, clear sign of his commitment, were always viewed by a few as the president's diversity folly.

In retrospect, beyond emphasizing the president's commitment, I have some doubt about the net positive effects of the appointments. I believe the appointees were unfairly stigmatized. Two of them were given responsibilities for which they had been inadequately prepared, and they had been assigned to supervisors who were unsympathetic at best. The third person, who reported directly to the president, fared much better with respect to supervisory guidance and mentoring. I became a friend of the student services appointee and provided advice and mentoring to him. But, I am firmly convinced that the one appointee who had a career goal to become a vice president and maybe eventually a president, had his growth and development stymied and his confidence shaken and that he would now be closer to his goal had that particular appointment never been made. Any minority person should be extremely cautious about accepting an appointment which results from utilizing an exceptional method. So called "opportunity hires" to increase minority faculty seem to be generally accepted even when not strongly embraced, especially if such a program has been enacted with faculty consultation and additional positions are provided for the minority hires. However, I think minority administrative appointments without the benefit of searches are fraught with problems. Such appointments are not in the long term interests of minorities. They begin stigmatized by suspicions about their qualifications.

My First Major Disappointment

I engaged in much contemplation and introspection before pursuing a position at a predominantly white university. I had many discussions with black and nonblack colleagues who were administrators or had been administrators at predominantly white institutions. I had invested much time reading the literature pertaining to the issues and concerns of black and other minority faculty, administrators, and students at predominantly white institutions. I had spent five years in a graduate school with few black students and fewer black faculty and a paucity of black undergraduates in the university. Therefore, I thought I could not be surprised by any eventuality. Was I ever wrong! About five months into my new position I was analyzing salary information in preparation for developing the next year's budget. To my great disbelief and utter amazement, I discovered that I was the lowest paid dean by far. Even though I had had five years of experience as vice president for academic affairs, and even though my college had over 70 percent of the students, credit hours, faculty, and departments, I made 12 percent less than the highest paid dean. That dean not only had less administrative experience than I, but was responsible for a school about one-fifth the size of mine. To add insult to injury, the dean of continuing education made 7 percent more. I did not know whether to feel angry, betrayed, or just plain foolish. I felt all these emotions, in varying proportions, depending on what aspect I was thinking about. Mostly, I felt foolish. I could not believe it and could not understand it. I was never provided an acceptable explanation. Surely everyone concerned knew that sooner or later I would see all of the administrators' salaries and note the discrepancy.

When the academic vice president had made the salary offer, I had asked specifically if he was confident that the figure was fair and appropriate in comparison with the other deans, considering the size and complexity of my college and my considerable prior experience. He had answered affirmatively without hesitation. The president had made the official appointment and salary offer. He was very much involved in my search and appointment process. In fact, he was more involved than anyone else because he considered the appointment of such importance. How could he have not been aware? I was sorely disappointed. Had I been wrong about the president's commitment to fairness and equity? Had I misjudged his integrity and his character? The years have confirmed that I was not wrong about the president's commitment, integrity, character, or his being an individual of high principles. But my confidence in the administration was seriously shaken at that time. My supervisor, the academic vice president, and his supervisor, the president, both expressed deep regrets about the mistake. They both committed to rectifying the situation as soon as possible, and it was corrected to my satisfaction. I never allowed that situation to affect my performance, behavior, or administrative relationships. Today, I still wonder why and how such a mistake occurred.

Personnel Issues: Appointments and Terminations

There is an established tendency of minorities to be concentrated in certain positions and in certain divisions at a predominantly white university.

Blacks and other minorities, especially Hispanics in California, are concentrated in student services, educational equity programs, human resources (personnel), community relations, groundskeeping, and affirmative action. When other offices have a disproportionate number of minorities, it is usually because of the efforts of the hiring administrator or the department chairperson. My dean's office at one point was comprised of all minorities: the dean (me), the associate dean, the administrative assistant, and a temporary secretary. There was no plan or desire to create a completely minority office, just a sincere commitment to increase the diversity of the university with competent people. When I searched for an associate dean of the college I called on all of my contacts to help me develop an applicant pool containing qualified minorities. My efforts resulted in appointing a highly qualified Hispanic. Some office staffs provided an image which belied the stated commitment to diversity and access. Some persons were bothered that the president's office staff did not contain an underrepresented minority. Should not the president's office reflect the university's commitment in such a practical, visible way? The same has been asked of other offices where there are two to four clericals and administrative assistants. Searches come and go in some of these offices, but the circumstance remains unchanged. Raising the issue produces instant defensiveness and sometimes resistance. Those of us who lead and demonstrate by example are often reminded of the limitation of such an approach.

One of the most important responsibilities any administrator has is the hiring of qualified personnel. And one of the most difficult and often painful responsibilities is nonreappointment or termination. There is an added dimension of difficulty if the administrator is a minority. If the appointment process results in a minority hire, one may very well be thought of as engaging in favoritism or "reverse discrimination," especially if the successful minority candidate is an internal candidate. If there are minority candidates in the applicant pool and the appointment is a nonminority candidate, minorities will likely be disappointed. The minority administrator my be viewed as lacking courage, of caring only for himself or herself, or of having sold out. The difficulty increases by several orders of magnitude if terminations are involved. A minority administrator may become involved even if the termination is not in his or her area of responsibility, because the dismissal of minorities is almost always a university matter, ultimately involving the president and all senior administrators.

During my fourth year, a black male faculty member was recommended to the president for nonretention as a result of the retention, promotion, and tenure process. The recommendation was supported by all four levels of review beneath the president. When this situation first began, I was a colleague of the dean of the school recommending termination. The dean asked for my advice and opinion with great concern. She was confident her decision was justified, fair, and necessary. Without taking issue with her justification,

I strongly urged that she reconsider. I pointed out that in light of our professed institutional commitment to diversity, in light of the faculty member's previous satisfactory reappointments, but especially in light of the fact that there were no examples in institutional memory of a probationary faculty member being similarly terminated, her position was extremely problematic and would eventually become untenable. I had similar conversations with the vice president for academic affairs and the president. The president essentially agreed with me, but I was not in the line of recommenders, I was a dean from another college. He felt compelled to sustain the four previous levels of recommendations, even though he doubted the decision would survive arbitration.

A year later, by the time the issue had blown up into a full-scale grievance with union representation, newspaper accounts, student demonstrations, and community action, I was the interim provost/vice president for academic affairs and had assumed responsibility for the grievance with assumption of that office. With the president, I met with the concerned minority community representatives. By that time, the matter had gone to arbitration. I assured the community that the faculty member would be treated justly and that neither the university nor the president had retreated from its multicultural mission. It was an extraordinarily awkward situation for me. Doubly so, because I thought it should have and could have been avoided. The outcome was as I had predicted from the outset. The faculty member was reinstated with pay and continued his probationary period. My credibility was bruised somewhat, but not beyond recovery. Some minority students, faculty, staff, and community members could not understand how I could have allowed it to happen in the first place. A few of them saw me as part of the problem, and fewer still understood my circumstances and the role I had played. The faculty union representatives credited me with playing a key role as the provost in resolving the issue quickly and equitably. Personnel issues involving minorities are always potential nightmares for minority administrators. One will likely "catch hell" from all sides.

Sometimes the hypocrisy I encountered became almost unbearable. Such episodes were almost always related to racism or sexism. I have learned through experience that an unconscious, seemingly unimportant decision that I make may be used as a rationale to support a decision by someone else that I would never support. About three years into my tenure as dean, an African American female who had served as a visiting lecturer was an unsuccessful candidate for a tenure-track position. I had provided the one-year position to the department for the temporary appointment. She appealed her unsuccessful tenure-track candidacy review. After examining the credentials of the finalists as well as her credentials, I found no basis to take the extraordinary action of overruling the department's selection. I offered the minority faculty another visiting lecturer appointment in another department in which she had a joint appointment and told her that there was a good possibility the position would be tenure-track in a year or two. She declined my offer and soon left the university.

The next year when a popular staff person in the administrative division was terminated, a concerned dean called a meeting and invited the other deans. The terminated person was erroneously thought by some to be Hispanic, and several deans were outraged by the decision of the division vice president, who was viewed as insensitive to diversity. As a dean, I was among the six academic administrators present. Several people expressed grave concern about the dismissal and decided to demand the reason for it. Someone proposed writing a letter to the vice president for academic affairs expressing concern about the termination of a minority person. That suggestion struck a nerve of one administrator, who did not desire to protest the termination on the basis of ethnicity, because she herself was in the process of terminating a minority individual. The hypocrisy that was evidenced in that meeting bothered me deeply.

As a result, I wrote my own memo entitled "The University and the Human Spirit" to the vice president for academic affairs to make my position clear on that and several other matters. Several excerpts which follow capture my tone and tenor:

> I am not presuming that you are unaware of the points expressed herein. However, I feel compelled to expand the 1/24 memo out of concern for my own credibility and moral posture. I am ever mindful of that powerful adage that people who live in glass houses shouldn't throw stones. I was also struck on 1/23 by the apparent lack of awareness of and sensitivity to the perceptions that are extant in this community. One colleague did not want to mention a concern for the treatment of minorities because she was involved in a process which could lead to the dismissal of a minority. Moreover, she assumed that I would have a similar view because I had already dismissed a minority. I was alarmed for at least two reasons. First, her conclusion that the dismissal of a tenure-track minority was the same as my not finding a tenure-track position for a temporary minority faculty. Moreover, she mistakenly harbored this view unaware that I had provided an option for that faculty person to remain employed full-time— an option which that person rejected. Beyond all that, why did not my colleague support an expression of concern for minorities irrespective of her own faculty personnel problems? If her decision was right and just, what is the basis of her objection? Secondly, I am concerned that the perception that I terminated a Black faculty member will give solace, if not encouragement, to others who dismiss affected-class minorities. After all, if Dr. Judson can dismiss a minority with justification, so can they. . . .
>
> As responsible and responsive administrators, we must understand that our actions may have great moment beyond our own offices and areas of responsibility. We must be aware of the implications of our decisions in the broader context of the University's welfare, mission, and image. Almost four years ago when I arrived, I found a Black community, distrustful of this University at

best. The University was viewed by that community as well as the Hispanic community, as racist, and unresponsive to the needs, hopes, and aspirations of minorities. The Black ministers communicated these perceptions to the President at our first breakfast meeting. Since then, we have made some progress, but years of neglect cannot be obliterated overnight.

Righteous indignation rings hollow, if those doing the fingerpointing have the same problems they criticize in others. We can be justly accused of hypocrisy if our own houses are dirty while we denounce the dirt in the houses of others.

There is much more I could say, but allow me to close with a few observations that have produced negative perceptions in the University community and broader community about our credibility, integrity, and commitment to a multicultural University.

- The President's clerical and support staff does not contain a single Black or Hispanic. When one walks into that Office the visual perception alone belies our professed commitment.
- We Deans complained that we were not told why Mr. "W" was dismissed, and we deplored the perception of shabby treatment. Yet, we have also not been told why Dr. "X" has been recommended for termination. It is a serious decision made even more serious by our recently adopted multicultural mission; by the critical underrepresentation of Blacks and Hispanics on the faculty; and by the intense, negative reaction that will probably be generated in the Black and Hispanic communities—especially in Stockton. The termination of a Black, male Ph.D. in the second year of probation may be viewed by reasonable persons as an act in the extreme.
- Two Black, female clericals in our area were terminated last year. The Deans on that occasion did not ask why or even express concern. We appear to be firing more Black clericals overall than we are hiring!
- There is not a single Black or Hispanic on the faculty of the School of Business. Yet, a Black part-time faculty who taught the Fall and Winter terms this academic year will not be hired in the Spring because there are no courses for him. Does not our commitment require a special effort in a situation such as this? Is it more ethical and moral to have no minorities than it is to terminate them?
- A Black, female faculty member undergoing review this year received departmental and University evaluations which raise grave concerns about her future, in spite of the overall recommendations for continuation. The department's evaluation can be viewed rationally as the initial step toward a 1990–91 termination.
- We have not provided, notwithstanding all of the discussions, set-aside faculty positions for 'opportunity hires' to increase affected-class minorities.

I do not absolve myself of responsibility for any of the above-mentioned or other concerns. I am not free from failings. I am, however, willing to confront the difficult problems with a view to finding solutions. I am willing to accept constructive criticism with a view to improvement. Dealing honestly with per-ceptions and/or realities can be very painful, but not as painful as denying them. I think the most effective response we can make is to become a model, to lead by example.

Affirmative Action Searches: Recruiting and Retaining Minorities

Service on search committees over a six year period has been an inter-esting experience. University-wide committees involved in national searches generally show broad and genuine support for principles of affirmative ac-tion, although there are always some skeptics. In my first year I participated in the search for an academic vice president. The committee was serious about its affirmative action efforts and endeavored to ensure that minorities and women received full and fair consideration. Sometimes their efforts went overboard and were a waste of time and even tried my patience, which is long-suffering under such circumstances. There were several Hispanic, women, and African American candidates in the pool. There was a general agreement to carry all candidates from underrepresented groups who met minimum qualifications through the first cut. It was clear to me, and at least to most of the others, that none of the African American candidates was moderately competitive and none had the experience for which we were looking. Yet a majority of the committee wanted to continue two or three into the later rounds. I believe their intentions were honorable. Finally, I spoke out and asked if anyone felt that either of the African American candidates had a "snowball's chance"! Since no one did, I pointed out the unfairness to the candidates of creating false hope by carrying them into the late rounds of the search. That seemed to have produced a sense of relief among my fellow committee members, and minority candidates who were clearly noncompeti-tive were dropped.

The committee was still very concerned to produce a slate of qualified candidates which was diverse with respect to race, ethnicity, and gender, which it did. Search committees which were narrowly focused, primarily composed of members from a single department or school, seemed less com-mitted to an affirmative action result than assuring that all legal and proce-dural requirements had been satisfied. I chaired a search for the deanship of a school where two prior searches had been unsuccessful. The third time around the school's representatives and faculty requested that I chair the committee. Unlike my previous experience, there was very little concern or talk about the underrepresented group candidates in the pool, although there were obviously some women and some Hispanic candidates in the pool. There certainly was no reluctance in the elimination of minority and women candidates in the earliest round. Little concern, if any, was expressed about producing a slate of finalists representing diversity. The finalists were all white males, although it should be pointed out that there were very few minorities in the pool and fewer still meeting minimum qualifications. The point is that no one seemed concerned other than me. When the group was narrowed to about fifteen candidates, there was still one Hispanic remaining, and he was not strongly competitive. Even that was too much for one member who remarked sarcastically that he guessed we need look no further since we had a Hispanic candidate. I responded that whomever we recommended would be qualified and if the successful candidate were a minority or a woman, so much the better, since that school had no underrepresented minorities on the faculty at that time. The successful candidate was a highly qualified white male, and I was credited with carrying out a successful search after two others failed.

I think that state policy mandating access and equity is likely to be more effective than federal regulations. There is legislative interest and often oversight. Accountings are often required during each budgetary cycle. If there is a commitment in the university system, that is even better. California was once such a state with an access and equity commitment by legislation. The CSU system had three core elements in its mission: access, equity, and quality. There were legislative mandates and system-generated programs to achieve the related goals. The system had at one time 40 percent minority students, 19 percent minority faculty, and 28 percent minority management and professional personnel. The campus where I was employed had over 20 percent minority students, 20 percent minority management and professional staff, and 9 percent Hispanic and black faculty.

There were a number of programs to attract and retain minority students and faculty. Beyond the familiar educational opportunity programs for minority students, there was a predoctoral scholarship program to encourage minority students to attend graduate school and a forgivable loan program for minority staff and faculty which provided up to ten thousand dollars to pursue doctoral degrees, as well as affirmative action research grants primarily for minority faculty and women. The only problem is that these efforts were modest at best. The programs were effective and positive but were oversubscribed for the limited funds. Such programs could be enormously effective if they were funded more generously.

Administrative searches conducted in my administrative area of responsibility or which I chaired were generally successful in producing minority and women finalists and minority or women appointments. Minorities, women, and proponents of diversity were pleased, but a growing vocal opposition was, of course, not pleased. I believe my efforts and the efforts of others demonstrated that with effort and commitment and some risk-taking, considerable progress could be made in increasing diversity. Many of us recognized that we had to put forth great energy and effort to solicit applications from minorities, to discover and encourage potential candidates who might not otherwise apply. In more cases than not, applicant pools can be developed with highly qualified minorities and women who can successfully compete on the basis of their qualifications solely. My appointment of a Hispanic woman to an associate deanship resulted from this aggressive approach. She would not have otherwise applied. In fact, she was not considering changing positions or entering administration when contacted. Another search I chaired produced a Hispanic associate vice president. There were members of that committee who told me later that had I not been the chairperson, it is highly likely that the appointment would have been a nonminority. On several occasions, the committee had to be reminded that our task was to produce a slate of qualified finalists, not select the administrator. I convinced them not to rank order but to provide an assessment of each finalist's strengths and weaknesses. In the end, there was unanimity that each of the finalists was qualified.

It has been more difficult to increase the number of minority faculty. Administrators can play a determining role in appointing administrators. However, the faculty is determining in the appointment of faculty. Administrators can still play an influential role in faculty appointments, especially minority faculty appointments. Great care and sensitivity are required of any administrator engaged in efforts to appoint minority faculty; this is especially true for minority administrators. One approach which appears generally to have the approval of faculty unions and at least the tolerance of some of the cynics of affirmative action is the "opportunity hires." Simply put, the president provides a few faculty positions to departments to recruit and hire minorities and women. These are additional allocations to the department and are therefore viewed as an incentive. The first problem at my former institution was the lack of such positions. During my first four years the institution was undergoing rapid growth while resources, although increasing, lagged behind growth. The next two years brought draconian cuts to our institution and our system. In short, in relatively good budgetary times and in absolutely horrendous budgetary times, we did not fund "opportunity hires." As dean of a large college, I developed my own opportunity positions out of my own budget. I ran the risk of being accused of using funds which should have been part of the normal allocations.

In general, departments which were willing to participate were provided with a position for a minority person. They were encouraged to hire ABD candidates as visiting lecturers. The appointments could become tenure-track upon completion of the doctorates. Departments which already had visiting lecturer slots allocated could convert them to tenure track for a minority faculty with a doctorate. I would also upgrade a position if necessary to attract a more senior minority faculty. Chairpersons were encouraged to request a tenure-track position if they could find and appoint a minority candidate with a doctorate. In one case, a department which had two years in a row requested a tenure-track position was finally provided one on the condition that a minority person be hired. This method produced eight minority appointments (4 Hispanics, 3 blacks, 1 Asian) in a university which had fewer than 240 full-time faculty. It is interesting to note that over the five-year period the regular faculty hiring process produced six minority appointments. We have known for some time that it is easier to recruit minority faculty where minority faculty already exist. It is difficult to predict the "critical mass" needed to bring about the enhancement effect. Unfortunately for us, our small campus suffered the fate of several larger campuses. Three of our minority faculty were subsequently hired away, two by sister institutions in the system.

On several occasions during my tenure at my previous institution I was asked about my faculty and administrative contacts at the HBCUs. I was asked directly if I knew of this kind or that kind of HBCU faculty member who might be interested in changing institutions. I have always stated flatly and unequivocally that I find such approaches unacceptable. Predominantly white universities should not, in my opinion, seek out black faculty and administrators, but especially black faculty, employed at HBCUs. Of course, if African American faculty and administrators working at HBCUs wish to respond to a position announcement, they have every right to do so, and then they deserve full consideration. Predominantly white institutions have an obligation to increase the number of qualified applicants in the pipeline, not take the easy way out by raiding. More recently, another trend is developing in which predominantly white institutions (PWIs) raid other PWIs for black faculty. A sister institution tried to hire away an African American faculty member after we employed the person at the ABD level and provided financial and release-time assistance for the completion of his doctorate and faculty development opportunities. Such a move may be beneficial financially for the African American faculty, but the overall situation is not improved.

Predominantly white institutions have an obligation to provide real solutions to the problem. They can recruit and employ African Americans and other minorities from nontraditional sources such as corporations and federal, state, and local government agencies. More important, they have an obligation to make a serious commitment to the long-term permanent solution. PWIs must recruit, enroll, retain, and graduate more minority students. They must provide academic and financial support for graduate study. They must hire their former minority students back as faculty. PWIs should then provide development and support mechanisms for the minority faculty. Faculty-faculty mentoring programs, in addition to previously mentioned programs, have proved to be successful. Administrative internships for African American and other minorities can serve as a vehicle for providing them with administrative experience and administrative on-the-job training. Positions such as assistant and associate deans, and assistant and associate vice presidents can be filled by those minority faculty with administrative internship experience. The assistant and associate positions can provide entries into the senior administrative positions at the same institution or at other institutions. I believe the key to increasing the number of senior African American administrators in the long term, is increasing significantly the number of African American faculty.

Backlash to Diversity

Efforts to promote diversity, multiculturalism, affirmative action, and civility on our campus are viewed by a small but influential group as impositions of political correctness. More than once, an appointment has been labeled as "reverse discrimination." At my former institution, one highly respected senior faculty member who would later become speaker of the University Senate, once remarked with deep sincerity that it was useless for a white male to apply for an administrative position, so, he was particularly pleased by the subsequent appointment of a white male as chief student affairs officer. I cannot help but believe that if the person had been a woman or minority and had the same qualifications in every respect, this faculty member would not have been as happy.

Admonitions to the administration against political correctness cropped up with increasing frequency over the past few years. There were times when the lack of sensitivity by advocates of diversity seemed to be acts of rubbing salt into the wounds of the noncommitted. During my first year at my previous institution I was taken aback by the president's announcement at the opening faculty meeting. He was very proud of the success of the affirmative action effort of the university, and he enthusiastically thanked everyone for contributing to the accomplishment. He noted with great emphasis a total of twenty-one new appointments—faculty, staff and administration—and only three were white males. I could hear low murmurs of disgust around me. Rather than focus exclusively on the positiveness of the women and minority appointments, he had focused, unintentionally, on the negativeness of not appointing white males. The next year the president proudly announced that we had had a most successful year: we had appointed all women and minorities; we had appointed no white males. After that I urged the president to never again relate our diversity accomplishments to the nonappointment of white males. It provided an implication of the white male as enemy. It constructed an affirmative action win-lose situation for white males. Feelings of "white male as victim" had been exacerbated by the president in my opinion. He agreed, thanked me, and never repeated that reference.

The risk of talking too much about progress in increasing diversity is that accomplishments are often exaggerated. Nonsupporters may develop a feeling of being overrun by minorities; or they may perceive that white candidates are being unfairly treated, especially white males. One very vocal, extremely harsh critic of the president seemed to exemplify such a perception of gross over-exaggeration. He was convinced, and stated publicly, that the president was blindly committed to diversity, especially with respect to Hispanics. He sometimes referred to the appointment of unqualified minorities. He wrote newspaper articles expressing his strong views. The supreme irony for me is that this person was one of my strongest supporters on the faculty. He gave strong public support for my candidacy for the deanship and for the vice presidency. He provided equally strong support for a Hispanic who was first appointed as an academic associate dean and then became a dean. In my opinion, as well as that of others, he is an outstanding faculty member. I believe he is honest in his stated views about me. Yet I am equally certain he is just as honest in his generalized statements about unqualified minorities being hired. Somehow he does not see the relationship between such statements and me and the Hispanic dean, and even though we have strongly differed several times, we remain good colleagues. Issues of race and ethnicity sometimes produce inexplicable and irrational views in persons who are otherwise admirable.

The perceptions by some people on the campus that we were moving too fast and by others that our progress was extraordinary were both illusions. Part of the reason for the misperceptions was the significant increase in minorities in the senior administration ranks from 1986 through 1990. In 1985 there were no minorities and only one woman in the senior administrative group comprised of the president, two vice presidents, two assistant vice presidents, one associate vice president, and five deans. However, by 1990, there were four minorities and two women (one woman was also a minority). The provost/vice president for academic affairs, dean of the College of Arts, Letters, and Sciences, and associate vice president for academic affairs were all minorities, and these are highly visible positions. The success in the administration was more than counterbalanced by slow progress in the faculty and staff areas, and most recent years of severe budget cuts have not been helpful. A typical student is very likely to graduate from the university without having a single class with a minority professor. Almost 90 percent of the department chairs and the majority of all administrators, including directors, are white males.

The Brown/Black Problem

The most difficult and painful issue which has confronted me is the brown/black problem. I have spoken with several of my African American administrative colleagues in the system, and it is a monumental concern to

them also. I had never before been in conflict with a minority group struggling for the uplift of their people through access, equity, and equal opportunity. Since 1990, there were times that I felt identified as the enemy by at
least a small group of Hispanics on campus. Even though my relationship
remained positive with the majority of Hispanics and even strong with a few,
I was hurt and puzzled by my treatment. The existence of a brown/black
problem was mentioned to me during my interview trip in 1986 by a white
administrator, and I took little note of the comment then. I was sure that if
there were tensions on my campus between Hispanics and blacks, I could
work with Hispanics to resolve the issues causing the tension, and upon my
arrival, I did not even remember the comment. I arrived firmly committed to
increasing the number of minorities in all constituent groups, but especially
increasing the number of Hispanics for obvious demographic reasons. My
initial relationship with Hispanics was warm and supportive. They welcomed
me and offered support.

During my second year, I attended a system-wide conference dealing
with the establishment of an institute to advance the education of African
American youth. Most in attendance were African Americans, fewer whites
and other minorities. During a small group session comprised of African
Americans I made some suggestion about input from Hispanics. I was simply
stunned when an African American male responded with intense vehemence,
"F—— Hispanics!" After a few moments of stunned silence I inquired into
the reason for his strong negative feelings. He willingly explained that Hispanics were interested in alliances when their own particular projects and
causes were addressed or their candidates were advanced, but that when we
wanted their support for our interests, instead of receiving reciprocity we
received a knife in the back. I offered that my experiences, though limited,
had been significantly different, that browns and blacks on my campus coop-
erated to advance their mutual interests in diversity and multiculturalism, that
we were friendly allies. He looked at me in wonderment and disgust, as if he
could not believe my naiveté. Nevertheless, I believed strongly in the validity
of my assessment. I concluded that he had had experiences which were very
exceptional. However, as I encountered more African Americans in the system, I discovered to my deep concern that his feelings were hardly uncommon. There were many, not necessarily a majority, who shared his views with
respect to Hispanics. I still could not accept such a scenario for my campus.

I thought my relationship with two of the four Hispanic faculty present
upon my arrival was particularly friendly. In my second year I asked their
assistance in finding Hispanic candidates for my associate dean search. I
appointed one to the search committee. Even though none of the Hispanics
on campus provided me with a single name of a potential Hispanic candidate,
I obtained names through other contacts. The search culminated with the
appointment of a Hispanic female. During that same year I was chair of a

search committee on which the other Hispanic faculty member served. He expressed admiration for my leadership and human relations skills, which were evidenced during the search. That search culminated in the appointment of a Hispanic associate vice president for academic affairs. In the meantime I was aggressively recruiting Hispanic faculty with some success. Later on, as provost, my recommendation was the determining factor in the appointment of a Hispanic male who was competing with a highly qualified African American female for an important administrative staff position reporting to the president. By traditional qualifications a strong case could have been made for the appointment of the African American. In my view, the Hispanic was qualified also, and he would provide the interpersonal skills and human relationship skills which the campus sorely needed, and I thought he would contribute to the campus beyond the responsibilities of his office. There were four interviewers for the candidates. There had initially been only three. I added, with the president's approval, the fourth interviewer, who was Hispanic. The two white interviewers strongly recommended the African American candidate; the Hispanic interviewer recommended the Hispanic, but noted that the African American was also well qualified. Had I recommended the African American, she would have been appointed. The president confirmed my assessment of the situation. From 1986 through 1991 the president stated, and I might add, accurately, that I had appointed or caused to be appointed more Hispanics to the faculty, staff, and administration than any other individual on campus, including the president. Hispanics in general acknowledged my commitment and my contribution. Then how did I become the "enemy" of some Hispanics?

At some point I became aware that to some Hispanics, a small group comprised only of Chicanos, appointing non-Chicano Hispanic faculty and administrators does not count. I was surprised to learn that the appointment of a faculty member of Cuban descent, and later an administrator from Venezuela, was viewed as minimally significant by this Chicano group. They were interested only in the appointment of Chicanos. The event which marked the beginning of the deterioration of the relationship was my appointment to the position of interim provost/vice president for academic affairs. Many people among the campus Hispanics, especially the activist Chicanos, and possibly some Hispanics in the local community, felt that the highest ranking Hispanic administrator should have received the appointment. This view was in conflict with the majority view of the overall campus community. The president, in response to a question, explained that an associate vice president who occupied a staff position did not "outrank" the dean of the College of Arts, Letters, and Sciences, a line position of major responsibility. Moreover, he pointed out that I had come with five years of experience at the vice presidential level. His critics were not mollified in the least. Matters became even more tense when that highest ranking Hispanic applied for the permanent position and he and I emerged as two of the four finalists.

The Hispanic faculty and staff had several meetings over the four-month search period to strategize and to galvanize support for their candidate. Initially, the meeting included some Hispanics who did not share the view that there was only one choice for the position; while they would have been happy had the Hispanic candidate succeeded, they would have been just as pleased had I succeeded. After a while the meetings involved those who would only support the Hispanic candidate. Some Hispanic students began to express the position of the Chicano group. The president was told that failure to appoint the Hispanic would be a clear indication of his noncommitment to increase Hispanic administrators. One Hispanic woman whom I had considered a friend, who had on many occasions brought baked goods to me, stopped speaking to me completely. She would not respond when I greeted her. The Chicano ally of my first three years refused to return my messages which were left with his secretary and on his answering machine. When I met him face-to-face, I asked him to come to my office because I felt we needed to talk. He agreed to come and then never showed.

The president received calls and letters imploring, if not demanding, the appointment of the Hispanic. The president described what was happening in the community as a political pressure tactic. He was disturbed that the participants would engage in such tactics or that they believed such pressure would work. Many on campus expressed to me on several occasions that they could not understand how the Hispanic candidate could reach the decision to apply for the position and how his supporters could treat with disrespect the most effective advocate at the university for hiring Hispanics. After a national search, I emerged the successful candidate. Ironically, my Hispanic competitor was the number two person on my staff when I took office. The small group of Chicanos continued to behave in the same vein, seemingly unperturbed by the counterproductive results of their tactics.

Near the end of the 1991 academic year, our president accepted a position at a midwestern university. The president had recommended me to the chancellor for the interim presidency. The Chicano group wrote the chancellor a letter urging that he appoint a Chicano as interim president and a Chicano to the permanent position and that he name one or two Chicanos to the search committee. They made it clear that a Hispanic who was not a Chicano was unacceptable. The chancellor also received a letter from the Executive Committee of the Faculty Senate urging that he not appoint an insider as the interim president and that the person appointed should not be a candidate for the position. The interim president was appointed from outside of our campus. He is a very respected, senior academic administrator from the central administration, who is very knowledgeable about and experienced in higher education in our system, state, and nation. My commitment to increase the numbers of underrepresented groups, especially Hispanics, remains unaltered. It is not easy for many, including of my some friends, to understand why. A commitment with a moral and ethical basis must be steadfast even if recognition and gratitude do not accompany resulting achievements. I am able to remain patient and undeterred because I understand the frustration, anger, and outrage of the dispossessed, oppressed, and excluded. I know why underrepresented groups, especially Hispanics, put so much value on each opportunity and why there is so much disappointment when that rare opportunity does not bear fruit.

The frustrations of some Hispanics are exacerbated by a lack of understanding of the stronger impact of national demographics on the way nationally searched administrative positions are filled. Some Hispanics often cite the 26 percent of Hispanics and 7 percent of African Americans in California as *prima facie* evidence that something is amiss about the relative success of African American candidates. They fail to realize that the percentages of blacks and Hispanics in the national applicant pool are the determining considerations. Moreover, a 26 percent Hispanic population at the state level does not translate to a 26 percent potential Hispanic representation in applicant pools even for searches limited to the state. Potential minority pools are determined by the number of minorities meeting the minimum qualifications, not on overall demographics.

The Ultimate Goal for Minority Faculty and Administrators

Mentoring is very important to the success of minority administrators. It is highly advantageous to have an effective mentor. It is also a responsibility for minority administrators to mentor aspirants in the pipeline. Some minority administrators are either so focused on their own survival or feel that serving as a mentor is too risky at their particular institution that they avoid serving that function. An African American dean at a sister institution related his disappointment at the refusal of an African American vice president to mentor him. I strongly advised him to find a non-African American mentor. While it may in some ways be more comfortable to have a same-race mentor, it is more important to have a mentor committed to helping you. I have served as a mentor to African American and Hispanic administrators. I share with them my experiences and try to help them avoid mistakes I have made. Sometimes I serve as a cheerleader and other times as a handholder. It is deeply gratifying to see others progress. African American administrators have an obligation to serve as role models and to contribute to the progress of the African American community, to return some small portion of that which we received from the sacrifices of others.

However, our primary responsibility is to succeed. Our success and our presence will encourage others and will help create an environment which may be more inviting and comfortable for African Americans and other minorities and more supportive as well. It would be folly to fail because of overextension of time and energy even in a good cause for the community. Such a failure would be tragic for the administrator as well as the African American community. The key is balance. We also must help the African American community understand our circumstances, our goals, and the demands upon us. I have been fortunate to have a very dedicated and knowledgeable mentor, a university president who happens to be a white male. He has given good advice, and he has been a steadfast friend. He has also learned from me. I have shared different perspectives with him about faculty matters and multicultural issues. It is also critical that a minority administrator be an administrator who happens to be a minority, that he be an administrator of all, responsive to all, fair and creditable to all. Your actions must confirm your position as an academic leader of all. I think it is also important that minority administrators and faculty refuse to accept a disproportionate responsibility and burden for diversity and multiculturalism. Diversity and multiculturalism are institutional responsibilities, not the primary responsibilities of minorities. Minorities should avoid being overburdened, while at the same time remaining faithful to their deeply ingrained, on-going historical commitment.

One difficulty confronting all faculty at comprehensive universities is satisfying the required heavy teaching load and the other criteria for promotion and tenure. The difficulty is exacerbated for African Americans and other minority faculty if there is additional pressure from colleagues, administration, and students relative to diversity issues. Many faculty are confused during the retention, promotion, and tenure process about the assessment of their scholarship. I know from experience of the inconsistencies from department to department, school to school, university committee to university committee. Minority faculty in a nonsupportive department or university can be especially vulnerable. They must understand clearly, academically, and politically what is required to achieve tenure and promotion and not be sidetracked by other solicitations of their time. Achieve tenure and promotion first; then you will have the opportunity and flexibility to give more time to diversity matters. The highest diversity and multicultural goal for a minority person is achieving tenure. That is a major contribution to the university and the students.

Overall Assessment

I feel strongly positive about my tenure at one of my previous institutions. I was fortunate to have had my initial administrative appointment at a predominantly white university, at that particular university rather than some others I know. I learned and grew and contributed. All segments of the campus, in general, responded positively to me and were supportive of me. My experience there was reaffirming and encouraging. To repeat, I recommend an approach to minority administrators that was recommended to me and which has served me well. Look for reasons other than racism to explain negative behavior. Assume and behave as if you will be judged on your abilities, accomplishments, and character, and most of the time, by most of the people, you will be. The overwhelming majority of people, irrespective of race or ethnicity, will relate to you on a basis other than color or ethnicity. And for the few who will not or cannot, ultimately, it will not matter.

CHAPTER 6

"A Dream Turned into Reality"

ALTHIA DEGRAFT-JOHNSON

Flipping through the pages of an inflight magazine, I came across in a particular article a comment that offered an interesting point of view: The comment was that "Some succeed because they are destined to; most succeed because they are determined to." Another phrase in the same article proclaimed that success is "a dream turned into reality." By many standards, I am considered to be a successful person. By my own account, I am succeeding at accomplishing my personal and career goals—I am turning my dreams into reality. However, whether the extent of my success is attributable to destiny or determination is arguable. To be sure, I have worked hard and long and have exercised a considerable amount of risk taking in my professional climb. Those facts notwithstanding, some of what has happened to me in creating this condition of succeeding has been beyond my control. I acknowledge the importance of other factors: being in the right place at the right time; having a willingness to explore new opportunities; maintaining an abiding belief that negative experiences have potential, positive outcomes; enlisting and accepting the assistance of others; and learning not to take myself—or others—too seriously.

Not only have discriminatory acts touched my personal life, but they also have entered my professional life. As in the case with other African Americans, I have encountered numerous discriminatory acts, and I have sometimes reeled in their aftermath. I have felt amazed by actions of people who have demonstrated outright, seeming oblivious attitudes while they have treated me as if I were less worthy of fair treatment simply because of the color of my skin.

I recall how disappointed I felt a few years ago when I was treated rudely by a minimum-wage store clerk with barely a high school education solely because of my race. This situation occurred after I had amassed much of what is generally considered necessary to succeed in terms of educational and professional accomplishments. I once again became aware that, no matter how much I achieve, I remain an African American first before other aspects of my being are considered. That condition carries more baggage than some are willing to admit. Still, I choose not to dwell on such negative situations. Discrimination defies logic.

Years of living and dealing with life's challenges and disappointments have taught me to appreciate Shakespeare's statement, "To thine own self be true." I also appreciate another set of words I heard some time ago, "Living well is the best revenge." These adages are important because I value truthfulness above all else, and I leave the attainment of revenge to others. My goal is to maintain a high quality of life that is personally and professionally satisfactory. The pursuit of revenge has no place in my daily operations.

The Early Years

During my childhood and adolescence, my parents protected me from many of the harsh realities of life for African Americans in this country. However, it is impossible for a person of color in North America to reach adulthood either untouched, unaffected, or unscathed by racial discrimination. The lives of far too many African Americans—and members of other racial and ethnic groups—have been violated simply because of race.

My early life was as insulated and provincial as those of most of my classmates, yet I differed from many of them in that I was ambitious and always maintained an outward view of life. I reached for a lifestyle about which I knew little and even less about how to attain. In fact, I identified my objectives long before I knew how to achieve them. At the time, they seemed to be grand dreams that disregarded any real or imagined barriers such as those created by racism. In retrospect, of course, I realize that the objectives were based on exceedingly limited experiences and were very narrowly defined.

Surveys have been taken in which Americans were asked where they were when President John F. Kennedy was assassinated. Many respondents were specific and clear in their responses due to the trauma that was associated with the event. The same is true of my first experience with discrimination that I recall clearly even now, over thirty years later.

The event occured when I was less than ten years old. My father took my older brother, my sister who is one year younger than I, and me to the Trailways Bus Station in my hometown of Morristown, Tennessee. We walked into the busy, brightly lighted waiting area which was filled with white passengers waiting to board the busses. All dressed in our Sunday best, we were very pleased to be taking a trip with our father to Knoxville to visit our grandparents. The entire trip was an adventure. I noticed that my father appeared uncomfortable upon entering the bus station. He looked around the room and said to us, "Why don't we go back here to sit down?" "Back here" was in the so-called colored waiting room in the back of the bus station. One of us voiced a preference to sit in the outer area; however, the insistence was slight when the faces of some of the white passengers stared uninvitingly toward us. My father never explained the reason that he "chose" to sit in a dimly lit room in the back of the building, and for some reason, we never asked. The answer was provided by retrospection.

I recall no significant acts of discrimination toward me in the seven years that followed, either while I was enrolled in my racially segregated elementary and junior high schools or while I was enrolled in the ninth grade in a school that was also segregated. I recall, however, that I was aware of problems between African-Americas and whites as racial problems were discussed, albeit quietly, in my community. African Americans spoke among themselves of "them" and what "they" were doing to supress progress by African Americans. In large part, African American women in my community were domestic workers; African American men were laborers. Because I was so ambitious, and in the light of the changing politics of race relations, I never expected that I would be required to become one of those women who cleaned the houses of white people or cared for their children. I understood the existing terms of employment as being a part of the status quo, yet I sensed a national undercurrent taking shape in the larger African American community. The activities of Martin Luther King, Jr., were gaining widespread coverage in the news. My parents gathered around the television each evening to watch the "CBS Nightly News" stories of the frequent boycotts and demonstrations. Daily news from Selma, Alabama, reached us. While I heard what was happening, I neither understood nor internalized it due, in a large part, to my age. I simply knew that people were protesting, fighting, and dying because they wanted to be treated fairly. The fact that they were protesting made me feel pleased and certain that I would not be required to suffer their indignities. Their dying made me fearful.

In 1964, the African American students in my community were given the option of attending either the racially segregated high school or the newly "integrated" schools with the understanding that in the next year we would be required to enroll in the racially integrated schools. I took that year to examine the new territory I would be entering—"the white high school," as we called it. Attention shifted to see what "integration" might do to us. The African American community watched with appreciable curiosity to see what might become of the African American teachers, staff, and administrators from the African American schools. We wondered what would become of those who showed great deference to whites via-à-vis those who were more separatist and less deferential in their behavior. What happened is that the principal of the African American high school, a physically imposing man, who, apparently, had made a few political enemies, was placed in the white high school as an English teacher. The principal of the African American elementary school, adept at telling whites what they wanted to hear, became the assistant principal in one of the formerly white elementary schools; others chose to remain in the newly created school for special education students which was now located in the historically African American elementary school. Members of the African American community whispered among themselves about the unequal assignments and noted that they had expected no more fairness than had been achieved.

My parents and other elders did not teach us about confronting discrimination. Feelings about unfair treatment were always registered in hushed tones or whispers among those in the African American community and through church sermons. Perhaps people were unsure of themselves given the changing environment that was created by the racially motivated protests. I was left to come to grips with resolving racially based conflicts and other similar situations through trial and error. Many times I was positive that I had been discriminated against as a result of my race; however, there were times when I found myself disadvantaged because some of the acts were skillfully masked to the point that proving discrimination was next to impossible. In the next six years, I fluctuated between ignoring discriminatory acts and confronting them. More often than not, I determined that the best recourse to the discrimination that I experienced was to ignore it. I felt angry when, for example, I walked into stores and either was ignored altogether when I wanted service or was followed as if I would steal. Yet I ignored the store clerks' rudeness as I did my shopping. My feelings were hurt when white teachers looked past me as if I were invisible, despite the fact that I had good grades and presented no behaviorial problems. Yet I ignored their treatment and studied so that I could make good grades. I knew that I was not inferior, as discrimination suggested; I also knew that I would have little to no assistance in reversing the discriminatory act.

As a result, I fully expected and was not surprised when white girls were exclusively selected to be cheerleaders because "black girls did not have rhythm," of all claims. Neither was it out of the ordinary that the children of doctors assumed the leadership positions in the Student Government or that the discrimination continued. The result was that I became socially detached and focused, instead, on all that I wanted to accomplish. I became clearly focused and driven to beat "them" at their own game, and I had some fits and starts in the process. Despite these shunts, however, I was treated well on the surface because I was a good student and was considered a person who was "going places." There always seemed to be a hollowness to the greetings and other exchanges from the white teachers. I craved a more intimate, personal level of caring and attention just as many developing students do. I resented the fact that I did not receive this attention.

Although he was less visible than some other national figures in the news in my hometown, Malcom X came to my attention. Like me, he was angry and was not about to take anything from anyone. In my view, he had the right approach. In my first year of college, I read his autobiography and was filled with disillusionment and awe at the same time. I was not enthusiastic about the fact that he had used drugs and had worked as a pimp. While I was not quite certain of what "reefer" was, I knew that it was not good, yet I remained attracted to him. I felt confused about whether I should take a pacifist approach as King was doing, seemingly to no avail, or whether I should use Malcolm X's direct approach. Confronting discrimination is an act of courage. The "CBS Nightly News" and local newspapers purposefully made a point of showing the consequences of confronting discrimination: bodies of African American men dangling from trees with white, hooded men standing nearby; a church where little girls' lives were blown away by dynamite; African American students who were turned away at the door of southern universities by governors, no less; and groups of African American men and women being beaten by National Guardsmen created a powerful message about what happened to dissidents. Few people were willing to step forward and speak out against overt or covert acts of discrimination.

But, ignoring discriminatory acts seemed not to yield the desired results for me. Neither did they make me feel good about myself. Initially, I was not inclined to present outspoken, direct dissent. Once in college, however, I felt that direct action was the best approach. I decided to adopt a style similar to Angela Davis', and my hair matched her Afro inch for inch, as if that mattered. Buoyed by youthful zest and ignorance, I determined that the appropriate response was to "tell off" anyone whom I felt was guilty of racially biased action and storm off in triumph. My plan was to confront the person with direct action—not the kind that would get someone killed—simply a good tongue lashing. I used this approach for a number of years, yet that approach proved unsatisfactory as well.

I decided to begin working with whites once again. It became clear that if I were on the outside, I had little likelihood of changing what was occurring on the inside. I recognized that with the verbal assaults I had shut down communication. Additionally, I considered the fact that many people with whom I interacted—who seemed to like me—actually did not like me. As a result of the pretense, however, they were able to gain access. It occurred to me, then, that I was needlessly isolating myself and, in effect, losing valuable contacts and opportunities to effect change. I learned to keep some feelings to myself, and later I learned to appreciate the saying, "Keep your friends close and your enemies closer."

Psychological Barriers

In zoos, some animals are controlled through the use of psychological barriers. At the Wild Animal Park in San Diego, for example, a six-foot gate is tilted inward at the top as a means of containing the Kenyan impala. Despite the fact that the impala could clear the fence easily, it does not attempt to do so because the inward-turned fence appears to be a ceiling above which the animal never attempts to rise. Another example can be seen in viewing the manner in which some elephants are restrained in captivity. Relatively small chains are fastened to one leg of these huge animals when control of movement is desired. When the elephant moves beyond the human's desired range, the slight tension stops the elephant from moving farther, and the elephant develops a limited range of motion, despite the fact that it could break the chain and freely go where it wants.

In colleges and universities, a similar phenomenon exists when senior positions are not held by people from minority groups. Students, faculty, support positions, junior administrative staff, and the community at large are effectively discouraged from attempting to push boundaries by the very absence of people of color in these positions. The psychological barriers are a result of widespread underrepresentation of minority groups in many senior-level positions, not only in higher education, but also in the larger society.

Opportunities and Minority Programs

Clearly, the person that I am today is a direct result of intervention and assistance provided by a few individuals and selected programs designed for minority asdvancement. It is important for me to note the private impact of programs targeted for minority groups. I acknowledge the value of such programs with regularity because of the current political milieu which threatens to eliminate racially designated federal scholarships and other programs that promote and support involvement.

As a child, I participated in programs sponsored by the Office for Equal Opportunity (OEO). During my adolescence, I participated in the Upward Bound program. As an undergraduate student, I received a minority academic scholarship. As a graduate student, I received a National Institute for Education (NIE) Research Fellowship designated for women and minorities. For a recent professional development activity, I received a Kellogg-American Association of State Universities and Colleges (AASCU) fellowship for supposedly upwardly mobile women and minorities. Each program has been instrumental in my personal and professional development. Politicians and other decision makers must recognize the importance of these programs that benefit people with potential to grow, but who may lack the means or knowledge of the inner workings and politics of organizations.

My childhood and adolescence occurred during the "War on Poverty." Several programs in my hometown operated as a result of funding from the OEO programs which provided jobs not only for several black men and women but also for children. Above all, I gained socialization skills and greater self-confidence. These programs were followed by the Upward Bound program. I was heavily recruited for the inaugural program because of my race, academic scholarship, borderline poverty status, and promise. Foremost, I benefited from the opportunities to travel without my family, I learned self-reliance that is gained from living away from home, and I received a firsthand glimpse of what college campus residential life involves. These were valuable experiences and opportunities for me and others in the programs.

Subsequently, other opportunities arose for me. Each time an opportunity was presented, I initially equivocated out of fear that accompanies youth and inexperience. Despite my ambition, I had a fair amount of nervousness about leaving the comfort of familiar surroundings. As a coping mechanism, I routinely reminded myself that the result could not occur without the initial effort. The exercise that I developed was to envision the worst that could result from engaging in the activity, determine how I would cope with that outcome if it should occur, and make the attempt. Overwhelmingly, I succeeded and moved on to the next opportunity. That approach continues today.

Challenges of College Life

My postsecondary experience began at Morristown College, a historically black junior college located barely five hundred yards from my home. Overly protective, my father expressed strong resistance to my going away to college. My older brother had graduated from the same college, so I accepted the dictum without realizing that it was subject to challenge. The fact that I had been more than mildly enthralled with the student life at the college made it easier to accept the compulsory attendance.

I was married at the end of my sophomore year and gave birth to a daughter the following year. I was extremely pleased with having a daughter. I realized, however, the complications that could ensue if I had other children while attempting to complete college and begin a career. At one point during the pregnancy, I was tempted to settle down, have additional children shortly thereafter, and remain in my hometown. A few cycles of soap operas, grocery shopping for the high point in my day, and other unchallenging activities quickly changed that fleeting thought.

That plan was changed also as a result of a conversation with one of my aunts. When asked of my plans following the birth of my daughter, I responded that I would return to college. She looked doubtful, but politely smiled. Not wanting to be viewed as "just another dreamer," I set out to follow through. Purely by serendipity, I learned that Carson-Newman College, the nearby Baptist college where I had earlier attended Upward Bound, had academic scholarships for minority students. I applied and received the scholarship that would support me through the two years that were required for me to complete a degree while my husband attended the same college on an athletic scholarship.

I have no fond memories of that experience. Only three faculty members took an interest in me and the other African American students who numbered less than 30 of the total student population of approximately 1,200 students. Unless we were athletes, we were virtually ignored. Fortunately, my husband was an All-American football player. The coaches attended to his needs with regularity. My family and small circle of friends comprise the basis of any fond memories that I might have of that experience because of narrow, conservative policies that do not recognize or appreciate diversity.

As an alumnus, I continue to have strong feelings of resentment and estrangement toward that college. The same insensitivity that was exhibited twenty years ago persists: A couple of years ago, I received an alumni newsletter. In curiosity, I leafed through the paper and viewed photos of white students pouring over books in libraries, strolling serenely on the campus, listening attentively in class, and enjoying social functions with college officials. The one student of color was an African American athlete who was photographed in the process of making a basket on the basketball court.

Beyond anger and full of dismay that the stereotypical representation was perpetuated, I immediately sent a letter to the president. In the letter, I explained not only the feelings of isolation that I had experienced as a student at that college but also my displeasure with the recurring stereotypical representation of the black male athlete. The attempt was to inform him of how the college could better serve students of color.

The president responded by glossing over the specifics I had shared with him of my experiences as a student. Further, he explained that the photo was only one of several shots of African American students that are routinely used in campus publications. He ended by referring my letter to the alumni director who also responded to me through an equally benign letter.

By the time I had written this letter, I had earned my doctorate and moved through several increasingly responsible positions since graduation some fifteen years earlier, and the Alumni Association had featured announcements in the newsletter. In her response, the alumni director referred in a congratulatory manner to my upward mobility and assured me of their commitment to diversity. A solution, of course, would have been for me to become involved in some way with the Alumni Association. In many cases, institutions invite their alumni who have achieved the type of professional advancement that I have to become actively involved in leadership roles. No such invitation has been extended to me.

The stereotypical photographs and exclusive practices continue. Not too long ago, I received a request for contributions to the Endowment Fund. Of four photographs on the cover, not one was of a person of color. I vacillate between fighting this battle and having my name removed from the mailing list.

Mentors and Role Models

I have had mentors and role models all of my life. They have been both relatives and nonrelatives, younger and older than I, males and females, blacks and nonblacks, and real and fictional. Some mentors have directly or indirectly consented to serve in that role; others have no awareness that I have used them, their advice, and examples to shape my life. I have also practiced self-advising and mentoring for a number of years.

Of the individuals who consented to mentor me, the common thread is that these individuals cared about me and my achieving my full potential. As for the others, the tie is that I was able to observe their actions and learn from their successes and failures.

Those who knew me well as a child justifiably considered me a shy, determined, firecely independent, aloof, and sometimes brooding girl. At the same time, my intellect was sufficiently respected by both my family members and the teachers in the racially segregated school which I attended to gain their support and frequent deference. In return, they held high standards and expectations for me, and I attempted to reach them. I would later come to do the same thing for myself. In some instances, I would set seemingly unachievable goals. Having shared them with others, I felt a certain obligation to achieve them, lest I be considered merely "a dreamer," and I did. The cycle became repetitive, habitual, and affirming.

Similar to the teachers at the racially segregated school, my teachers at the desegregated school to which I was eventually required to transfer found me equally worthwhile, "for a black student." In turn, they too supported me in a closet fashion, and I had the critical ingredients for success: supportive family members and others willing to serve as mentors and role models. My potential was recognized, nurtured, and developed; my successes became others' successes.

The persons significant in shaping me are my father, mother, ninth grade English teacher, and high school music teacher. Each was well aware of the desired outcome, and I draw upon their early advice and role modeling even today. Ironically, each person's objective complemented and balanced that of the others without prior consultation on their part, no doubt.

My father, who values debate and competition, seems to have desired me to be a person who is able not only to form an opinion but also to exchange points of view in a competitive manner. Winning is important to him, especially in the face of negative circumstances.

My mother, who values human relations, consistency, and persistence, seems to have desired me to be a person who can have an opinion, but be able to listen to and synthesize other views. Even when the odds seem overwhelmingly stacked on the opposing side, she encouraged persisting through to completion.

My English teacher, who valued African American literature and oratory, seems to have desired me to be a person who appreciates the value of her heritage and, feeling pride in that past, publicly presents herself and the literature of other African Americans in a cogent manner.

My music teacher, who valued the visual and performing arts, seems to have desired me to be a person who can appreciate aesthetics and the fine arts and is able to use them to achieve balance in life.

All of these persons sought to instill self-confidence and a strong responsibility for ethical behavior. Had I not had the support of family and a few close mentors, I doubt that I would have been able to deal effectively with life circumstances in general, and in higher education, in particular.

Without exception, the expectations and support of others led me to conclude that I could succeed at whatever I wanted—race and sex notwithstanding. A tacit assumption in my family was that my siblings and I would earn college degrees. Each of us did, and all but one of the six children have graduate degrees. We were and continue to be competitors, support systems, and role models for each other.

The Career Path

The manner in which I chose education as a profession is perhaps similar to that of others in my age group. People who seemed to enjoy lives of comfort in my community were teachers and others who worked in schools. The teachers, safety patrol officer, and other school staff all lived in nicer neighborhoods than I. They were regarded as "professionals," and their children all seemed to be special. Of my family members who were not laborers or ministers, the one profession that was pursued was education. It seemed natural to me that if I were to become a "professional," my profession would be teaching. Little regard was given to what I could become if all stops were removed and the opportunities were limitless. The truth is, barriers were plentiful, and opportunities were not limitless. Nevertheless, opportunities existed, and I had no plans to ignore them. I quickly realized what I wanted, and I set out to get it.

My career in higher education spans a twenty-year period, nearly eighteen of which have been in approximately two-year stints, except for my most recent position. I moved often because it became clear to me early in my career that the only means by which I would progress would be to move from one institution to another in increasingly responsible positions. The politics of race and gender have created a ceiling in most colleges and universities that only a few have been able to surpass. I know of no women of color who have moved from entry-level faculty positions to senior administrative institutions within the same institution. If such a phenomenon exists, it is the exception rather than the rule. I was aware that I would be viewed by many as a "job hopper" and that moving so quickly from one position to the next carried significant risk; however, the potential benefits outweighed the risks.

Upon graduating from college, my first job was teaching in the same historically black junior college from which I had graduated only two years before. I taught developmental English, composition, and a survey of literature. I was offered the position despite the fact that I did not hold a master's degree because my husband had been appointed as the recruiter and coach.

My bachelor's degree is in sociology with an English minor, and I immediately began a master's program at the University of Tennessee (UT) with urging and initial financial support from the college's president. Clearly, I needed better credentials to teach in a college. Having done student teaching for a high school sociology class only months before, I eagerly decided to do what was necessary to teach on the college level. I was told by other students that blacks were not welcomed in UT's English program, and desiring to complete my master's degree with as little hassle as possible, I opted for the English education program.

Upon my completion of one-half of the master's program, the president withdrew his support, indicating that it was not important to him if I earned an advanced degree. At this point, I had committed sufficient time and energy to take on the funding myself. I completed the program eighteen months after I had begun it while working full time. I immediately left my employing institution, moving to a community college located nearly four hours away.

The move occurred before two-location families were in vogue to the extent that they are today. The lure to advance my career was too great to let minor obstacles divert my plan for upward mobility. It was the beginning of a pattern of employment that resulted in my consistently changing locations at two-year intervals for the sake of career advancement.

I had scarcely been teaching English at the new community college for one quarter when I was offered the position of director of personnel and institutional research. I was flattered by the offer, attracted by the salary, and optimistic about learning the associated tasks. I accepted the position despite the fact that I did not have a clue about what the job entailed. As I considered the situation, I was certain that I would learn how to do the job; I did.

For many years, I took positions without so much as a hint of what the jobs involved. That inexperience hardly dampened my ambition or risk taking, however. My plan was clear: I would take the position, learn as much as possible, draw upon others for support; and leave the office and institution in better condition than I had found them. That is the scenario that played out in this particular job before I left it at the end of two years to venture into private industry.

I took the position of assistant personnel manager at a major clothing manufacturer for no reason other than ambition. The location was two hours closer to my husband, but that was not actually a consideration. The thought of joining the jet setters who moved effortlessly from Tennessee to San Francisco and beyond appealed to me. It was an offer I could not refuse.

As a student working during the summer, I had worked as a cashier in neighborhood grocery and variety stores. Unlike some of my sisters, brothers, and neighbors, I had never set foot in a factory. This was not because I was opposed to the idea—I could not pass the physicals because I was often anemic.

The factory environment was new for me, but not untenable. The issue of greater concern for me was the fact that I was insufficiently challenged. In retrospect, I can identify the problem as being twofold: (1) I was brought into a management development program without being told so, and (2) no one articulated to me the reason why I was hired, gave me mentoring, or explained what I was to do in broad, sequential terms. I was simply told that I was expected to learn the operations and to observe how business was conducted on and off the manufacturing floor. Perhaps the explanation should have been enough; however, without a better sense of where I fit in, these activities were not meaningful.

To have been most effective, it would have been helpful if I were one of the "good old boys" who could drop in the men's lounge and sit around telling fish tales and war stories; however, none of this was clear to me before taking the job. Shortly after my arrival, I was clear on one thing only: I was not challenged, and I often felt that I was there to serve as the resident black person—the company seems to have had an affirmative action show cause requirement. I felt this way because my office was immediately visible upon entering the company's administrative offices. Having recently read the experience of "The Spook Who Sat by the Door," I was convinced that my role was similar. Whether that was actually the case remains a subject of conjecture. I left that position after only six months and returned one month later to school to begin studying for a doctorate.

On several occasions, the president who moved me into administration heard of my interest in obtaining a doctorate. During those conversations this president, my first professional mentor in the business of higher education, encouraged me to get the doctorate in higher education administration. Recalling that advice, I entered the Educational Administration and Supervision program at UT. I worked on the degree while concurrently holding an NIE

Research Fellowship designed for women and minorities, teaching English in a nearby historically black collge, and raising my daughter now as a single parent. The college failed to meet the payroll two times too many, and I left the job to accelerate completion of the degree.

While working on my degree, I explored the department to get a sense of university practices and politics. I interviewed several faculty before selecting one to serve as my major advisor and to chair my dissertation committee. We determined the courses I should take, and I set out to meet the requirements. Each time I became closer to completing them, he changed the requirements. After considerable effort, I finally was able to get him to commit in writing to the courses I was required to take. It seems that I was moving too quickly through the program.

I was elected by my cohort group to chair our residency seminar for a quarter. The election was unexpected, yet I appreciated this action. All went smoothly as I concurrently worked through my dissertation proposal. Upon presentation of the proposal to my committee chair, I learned of a problem with his expectations. One of my committee members informed me that the chair did not want to approve the proposal because he felt that it was "too clean." This committee member indicated to the chair that the proposal should be "clean" because I was an English major and I was obviously intelligent. The chair remained unable to accept the fact that I was able to do the work as well as I did. I helped him to resolve his problem by relieving him of his responsibilities as my chair and easily found someone to replace him. I was later informed that no doctoral student had ever done that before. It could have proven to be political suicide; however, I graduated in short order. I completed the degree two years after I began the program.

Upon graduation, I set out to find out what career I wanted to pursue. I applied for and subsequently received a lecturing position at Abyero University in Kano, Nigeria. I packed up my daughter and my most cherished belongings to embark on a two-year stay. A few complications which perhaps would have been resolved over time caused me to return home after only a very short stay.

I returned to my hometown and took a position at the community college as assistant director of the college's Off-Campus Center. I was responsible for varied administrative tasks required to operate the center, and I taught English composition. The director was a former military person who cherished the military way of doing business. I did not share his enthusiasm for that method of operation and felt free to let him know of my different opinion.

His position came open in my second year. I was not encouraged to apply. He informed me that I would not be selected for the position because of reasons unknown to me even today. I found the entire situation bizarre and disheartening. If I were not able to move from the assistant director's position to that of director, I saw no future in the job. I left at the end of two years.

I worked in Augusta, Georgia, as an English faculty member for nearly two years before moving to Syracuse where I lived for four years. My experience as an assistant director to the Tennessee off-campus center director helped me receive a position in a community college in upstate New York. I held the position of director of the extension center for two years and had my first real experience supervising faculty and staff and overall administration of a unit.

After two years at the community college, I decided that I wanted to work in universities. I had only a narrow network, so much of my advising and mentoring was self-directed. My greatest direction about career options came from *The Chronicle of Higher Education*. I used the *Chronicle's* bulletin board to review position responsibilities first; I then matched them with my experiences. By this time, I had identified my career goal as president of a college or university, and I wanted to gain exposure to the operations in a president's office.

I was appointed to the position of executive assistant to the president in an upstate New York university. During the interview, the president asked me about the reasons for my interest in the position. I informed him that I wanted to learn about what goes on "behind the door." In other words, I wanted to gain exposure to the politics of higher education and to learn how decisions are made. It was one of the better career moves I have made. I gained the experiences I sought and improved my leadership skills in the two years that I held the position.

The president seemed to have a sincere interest in helping me to meet my professional goals. He provided me with experiences that would allow me to get a sense of how higher education works, although initially, he was reluctant to include me in some higher level discussions and events.

Doing things well was important to the president and to me. He quickly opened doors for me once he was certain that I would not embarrass him or the university. I recall, for example, that I was coordinating planning for the first university convocation. When the selection of music was discussed, I worked with the Media Services staff person and selected Vivaldi's "Four Seasons." The president and I sat down to go over the plans, and he learned that I had selected the music. He was visibly uncomfortable. I asked about his concern, and he seemed embarrassed to admit that he was concerned about the music. I assured him that the music would be fine, and he relented. In jest, I have speculated whether he thought I might have a recording of Aretha Franklin or rap music in the background to distinguish the occasion.

On the day of the event, the president, visiting chancellor, and faculty entered the room armed to the teeth in academic regalia. As the chancellor began his remarks, his first comment spoke to the musical selection. He indicated how refreshing it was to participate in a processional that did not rely on the old stand-bys and expressed his fondness for Vivaldi. The president and I exchanged glances, and I felt victorious. We learned to relax around each other. In many ways, my position served the same purpose as an internship.

At approximately the same time, the president and I agreed that I had outgrown the position. I realize that some other considerations were involved in both our decisions; however, I was ready to move to an increasingly responsible position. I talked with the president, who shared information that indicated that the career path for presidents is often through academic affairs. Again, I scoured the *Chronicle* to determine what my next move might be. I read the position descriptions and decided that I wanted to do the work of an assistant/associate vice president for academic affairs.

In one search where I was a semifinalist, I was eliminated due to my race. One of my referents, a white woman, informed me of her telephone conversation with a university official. As they discussed my credentials, he seemed favorably impressed with me. He then asked if I am black, and she answered in the affirmative. He stated, "Well, we don't have many of those around here." She was more angry than I would have been.

I accepted the position of assistant vice president for academic affairs at a midwestern state university comprised of 16,000 students and 750 faculty members. The university was ever on the brink of dissent, change, and opportunities to grow and make a significant contribution to higher education. However, in-fighting, inbreeding, parochialism, and an outright resistance to change were in abundance. Persons of color were noticeably absent in faculty, administrative, and student populations, and in the greater community population of 60,000.

I took the position despite my feeling that it was not in my best interest to do so. Isolation was a consuming fact of life for most persons of color who lived there. For me, the isolation was intensified because I was a single senior administrator.

By its very nature, senior administration carries isolation and separation from those in junior positions. The challenge is exacerbated by adding conditions of singlehood in a small town that is primarily comprised of families. Also problematic is the addition of race where the particular racial group is overwhelmingly underrepresented in a setting that is located eighty-two miles from an urban area.

The university was no place for the faint of heart. I attempted to find another job in my first year, but I was unable to without having to move backward, careerwise. It seemed that I was required to serve the time. In fact, I viewed my tenure there as a condition that I was required to endure if my career was to be protected. I dealt with that experience for four years by developing relationships with a select group of people, all from the "outside" whom I continue to regard as friends. In addition, I realized that I had to leave for an urban area every fourth weekend.

Shortly after arriving on campus, I heard that statements had been made that I had been appointed because of my race. I had long ago decided not to entertain such discussions—for years whites have been selected for positions because of their race. This practice only becomes problematic when persons of color are involved.

In my experience, I have seen such discussions detract a person from doing the job to the point that the low expectation becomes a self-fulfilling prophecy. I took the position that I would do the job well and that my record would speak for itself. My approach proved valid when I was eventually sought out for advice from some of the very people who had criticized my appointment as being racially based.

The issue of invisibility was constant both on campus and off. The irony is that, while I was highly visible by virtue of both my position and my color within the university, I often became invisible when taken out of context. One day when I was in Washington attending a meeting, I passed the university president on the street. For two years, we had held offices located next to each other and had seen each other nearly daily. When we approached each other on the street, however, he showed no sign of recognition of me. I immediately recognized him; however, I chose not to stop and greet him.

My previous position was vice president for academic affairs at United States International University in San Diego. This is a position that I held since April 1994, and I feel that both the institution and the position were perfect fits for me at that point in my life and career.

The university is comprised of approximately three thousand students who study at the San Diego campus as well as our universities in Nairobi, Kenya; Mexico City, Mexico; and a center in Orange County, California. As the chief academic officer, the position carried far-reaching responsibilities and opportunities. I came into this position fully aware of how to do the job, and I felt challenged and supported by a group of professionals who had the interest of the university foremost in their work.

I was responsible for ensuring academic quality on a domestic campus as well as two international campuses. My colleagues and I worked together to position the university to be a leader in international education. Our vision was shared and promising.

I thank my parents for their support. My daughter is completing her senior year at the university and is intelligent, sensitive, ambitious, and balanced. Clearly, living well is the best revenge.

CHAPTER 7

All American Dream/African American Reality

WESLEY HARRIS

When does the meaning of racism first appear in one's life and what impact does it have on that life? In my youth, this was the quintessential question. Today, this question no longer dominates my attempt to resolve my experiences and to understand more firmly what life in America is. An answer or response to this question does not provide useful information to advance an assertive African American scholar. At best, an answer to this question would address white racism as an external agent, external to the finite qualities possessed by creative scholars, leaders, and managers of African lineage. Hence, from a perspective of gaining useful information, this question is not well posed.

The questions that are critical at this time may be stated as follows: How does one overcome the adversities invoked by racism and not allow its ignorance to influence one's destiny? What enables one to remain motivated in a society that does not recognize the total contributions and capabilities of African Americans?

As I was a young child growing up in Virginia, there was a special emphasis placed on education. My parents, like many African American residents of Virginia, were tobacco factory workers. This strenuous work greatly increased the chances of premature death, especially among the African American men, which left many of the women to become the sole providers of their families. This situation occurred in my case, and because of the early death of my father, my mother not only accepted the role as provider, but with the assistance of my grandmother, aunt, and sister, also served as a motivational force in my educational career. I credit these strong African American women as being the dominant inspiration in molding me into the individual I am today.

I was fortunate enough to have mentors at school as well as at home. All of my high school instructors were African Americans, and many of them possessed master's degrees, which was the degree held by many college instructors at that time. Faculty positions at the historically black institutions were difficult to come by, and because of racial segregation, black faculty were not allowed to teach in Virginia's white universities. This situation proved advantageous to me because, through their disciplined teaching, I was encouraged by those instructors to excel and achieve, regardless of society's ignorance. There was no question I would attend college, for I was told many times that this academically and socially broadening experience would provide opportunities that would otherwise not be afforded me. Aware of the injustices inevitably faced by people of color, I prepared myself by ensuring that I had the best education possible.

I began undergraduate school in 1960 at the height of the civil rights movement and in the very first wave of postsecondary desegregation. It was difficult being one of few African Americans at a predominantly white university. Although my initial intent was to receive a bachelor's degree in physics, due to the state laws, I was allowed only to pursue a degree in aeronautical engineering. (In the 1960s African Americans were not allowed to study physics at the white university in the state in which I lived.)

Having gained the status of a student at a predominantly white university certainly did not harbor me from the racial tension that existed outside the campus. African American students were still segregated in public areas. This injustice encouraged me to become politically active in campus protests. With the support of a few faculty members, I became actively involved in campus civil rights activities. With their support, I joined a sit-in at the campus theater where African Americans were only allowed to use balcony seats. I also protested at a posh restaurant that restricted African American patronage. My protests included condemnation of segregated undergraduate and graduate activities on the university campus as well.

Upon earning my baccalaureate, I moved on to graduate school. While studying for my doctorate, I continued to protest against racial discrimination. This action was taken with the intent of creating a more diverse environment on one of America's leading university campuses. I made a conscious effort to meet informally with the university's president on ways to provide a more wholesome environment for African Americans by employing more African American instructors. When I completed my academic studies, I believed that I had been adequately prepared for the challenges and opportunities that lay ahead. The degrees that I held were received from some of the country's most prestigious universities, but the challenges I faced as an African American professional were more dynamic than I had anticipated.

After several years of research and teaching, I began the administrative phase of my career at a large state-supported university in the Northeast where I found myself constantly harassed by junior officials. For example, as a senior administrator I traveled frequently, using university vehicles, but I was always required to provide my driver's license as proof of my position. I inquired about this situation among white administrators and found that they were not required to present their driver's licenses but were issued the use of the university cars at their discretion, without question. On one occasion when I requested transportation through the vehicle pool, I was actually denied authorization. Although I was obligated to attend a university engagement which was several hundred miles away, I was told that access to a university vehicle was unnecessary. By this time, I had become well acquainted with the climate in my working environment. I was convinced that there would be many roads paved with the same, if not worse, indignities. This realization became a catalyst in my road to success, for I approached these injustices as challenges, rather than as obstacles.

Later in my administrative career, as vice president in a white, southern university, I also witnessed many negative situations. Unfortunately, in the South, even as late as the 1980s color reigned supreme in the minds of white southerners. The double standard was constantly present, and educated African Americans received little, if any, respect for their accomplishments. I remember vividly an incident involving the (university) president's wife and one of my faculty colleagues who was an African American woman. It was football season, and the professor, like many of the university's diehard football fans, had spent most of the season following the team to each game. The president and his wife also supported the team by attending each game. When the president's wife took note of the professor's interest in the team, she asked, "Are you following the football players to provide services?" The president's wife assumed that because the professor attended the games unescorted by a gentleman, she was obviously yielding sexual favors to the players. Along with this kind of base assumption, there was also a blatant disregard by the university's faculty for African American students as serious contributing scientists, engineers, and scholars. While incompetence and inexperience were not tolerated of African American students, these qualities were totally accepted in the white males and females who were being molded to become future southern leaders. After becoming aware of this unethical policy, I endeavored to make considerable changes in the university's cultural makeup.

Through my efforts to promote justice and equality at the university, I eventually exposed a notable white professor who had allowed several white students to use his research documents in obtaining graduate degrees. Evidence of this unethical action was produced by a graduate student who observed a similarity between a former students's thesis and the professor's research document. When both documents were examined, it was discovered that they were identical. The former student involved in the episode was a government employee with financial influence over the professor's research endeavors. When the matter was investigated, it was revealed that many other students also had used the professor's documents in obtaining graduate degrees, including doctorates, in exchange for research grants. The professor denied the accusations and, because of the notoriety of the incident, resigned from the university. The students involved were reprimanded in only a few cases, while still operating in full capacity at their places of employment, This unfavorable exposure was publicized across the country in various newspapers. Although an accurate description was given of the incident, the newspapers could not describe the hell that followed for me. From that point forward, I experienced a great amount of vicious, overt racism.

In higher education, an African American man refuting the word of a southern, white man is still virtually unheard of in the South, although such an action is permissible among other white men. Because of this philosophy, a small conspiracy was created against me. I felt I never had the full support of my superiors at the university and that they were aware of the professor's crime before my arrival, but had hoped the problem would go away and eventually resolve itself.

As a result of my revelation, I was forced to deal with many degrading accusations. I was accused of being a hypocritical, lying, self-serving manager who managed by terror and intimidation. I was deemed incompetent, although I had published more technical papers than anyone at the university and possessed a notable degree from an Ivy League university. However, many of my colleagues possessed degrees from undistinguished universities and mediocre records of achievement. I also was accused of being unfamiliar with my faculty and staff. This accusation seemed ironic, for I knew each employee.

Continuing with my duties as administrator, I did not allow these indignities to deter my efforts for equality and excellence. I utilized my authority by incorporating programs and giving annual financial awards for exemplary performance that proved advantageous to the staff. My endeavors were accepted and implemented, though with questions from the senior staff. I felt my contributions were most beneficial and would remain intact regardless of my status at the university. Unfortunately, these feelings were not shared among my peers.

Soon after my departure from the institution to accept a higher level position at another university, I was written by one of the university professors. Surprisingly, he congratulated me on my recent appointment and complimented my previous style of administration. Then he explained in his letter a set of decisions that had been made in one of the faculty assemblies. All of the programs I had implemented were immediately eliminated in an attempt to erase all traces of my involvement with the university. The ignorance and hatred were so intense that, the staff was willing three months after my departure to deny themselves awards and opportunities that would enhance their career objectives.

Although our struggle for equality remains just that, a struggle, I am thankful for the knowledge and peace of mind that it takes to advance in today's society. I pride myself on being a strong advocate of equality and someone who stands firm on his decisions. Every day brings a new challenge, but I welcome these challenges with the hope of encouraging others and instilling in them the values I was so fortunate to receive. The road to success is not an easy one, and for African Americans there are definitely no short-cuts. However, with determination and encouragement from others, each person is capable of achieving and contributing to society.

Out of the Mainstream: An Unorthodox Pathway to the Office of Graduate Dean

BARBARA SOLOMON

I love my job! This is not a statement that an administrator in higher education is frequently heard to make. The cultural norm in the academic community prescribes that a senior-level management "position" should never be referred to as merely a "job." Yet the academic attitude regarding administration is patently ambivalent. Deans, provosts, vice presidents and presidents, are accorded a certain level of prestige, since universities are in some ways as hierarchical as churches or the military. Yet most faculty consider the lives of the people at the top to be a constant confrontation with hemorrhaging budgets, staff discontents, meddling alumni, and problem-generating physical plants. If this characterization of university administration were true, I would have found little to love; but instead I have found intense gratification from the opportunity to see the "big picture" of higher education, to contend with shifting canon and paralyzing moral dilemmas and to engage in creative problem solving. Although higher education administration does not entirely suppress the yearning for a more unfettered life of the mind, it has its own intellectual and emotional compensations.

I am an African American woman, formerly a part-time professor of social work, and a full-time dean of graduate studies in a predominantly white but increasingly multi-ethnic university. In my case, the discovery of the potential for satisfaction in university administration came late and the pathway to the deanship was circuitous. From the time I received my Bachelor of Science degree in psychology from Howard University until the time that I was appointed acting dean of the Graduate School in the University of Southern California, more than thirty turbulent, momentous years have elapsed.

In the years between, I received a master's degree in social welfare, spent seven years in professional practice as a clinical social worker, three years completing the doctorate in social work, and twenty years climbing the ranks of the faculty. The question posed here is: To what extent has racial or gender discrimination influenced the trajectory my career has taken or settled its course for the future?

In order to answer the question posed, it is necessary to consider my "case." In the context of health and human services, it is not considered particularly creditable to be a case. However, from the perspective of social or behavioral science research, the case is a significant unit of observation. The thorough description and analysis of the case is one method available to the researcher interested in developing insights about human interactions and generating hypotheses for further study. However, there are several difficulties in adopting the case study method to determine the effects of discrimination on the careers of minority administrators in predominantly white institutions. The first is the problem of demonstrating that an alleged act of discrimination against minorities has not in fact been experienced by others who are nonminority. A second is the problem of the interaction of multiple sources of discrimination or bias. Even if it is suspected that a promotion of a faculty member to an administrative position was made on the basis of some factor other than merit, it would be difficult to determine whether that factor was race, gender, the relative prestige of the candidate's discipline in the academic hierarchy, or some idiosyncratic preference of that particular academic institution.

Despite the difficulty in pinpointing the sources of bias or even accurately confirming it in the first place, the single case study can suggest the manner in which factors other than merit, such as racism and sexism, may interact to influence careers in higher education. The desired outcome is not to discover some type of linear cause-effect relationships between the independent variables of race, gender, class, or academic discipline and the dependent variable of upward mobility. It is rather intended to heighten sensitivity by expanding perceptions of the possible. It is to reduce the likelihood that we will jump to conclusions about whether racism or sexism is or is not a factor in decisions we make about curriculum, student admissions, faculty recruitment, or the allocation of resources. In my own case, a "critical incident," can serve to illustrate the multidetermination of upward mobility, including perhaps the possibility that institutional racism should be included as one of the determinants.

A Critical Incident

A faculty member once said to me, "No matter how many perquisites we faculty have to give up, we should hold on to the sabbatical as a divine right, never to be bargained away." The sabbatical leave is indeed a hallowed suspension of the academic routine, which, if used well, can be highly productive and rejuvenating. When the benefits of faculty sabbaticals are weighed against their cost to the institution, that cost appears to be almost negligible. After teaching for six years in the School of Social Work, I was scheduled for my first sabbatical leave and was not sure how I wanted to spend it until I received a brochure announcing a one-year program in higher education administration. The Claremont Colleges had received a grant from the Carnegie Corporation to conduct the program to provide management training especially for women in higher education. According to the announcement brochure, a program of this kind was needed because of the paucity of women at senior administrative levels and the lack of opportunities for women to develop the skills needed to serve effectively as dean, vice president, or even president in a college or university.

As a child growing up in Houston's fifth ward in the forties and fifties, I was familiar with the nature of the work done by teachers, ministers, librarians, nurses, doctors (from personal contact), and even lawyers, psychiatrists, airline pilots, and professional athletes (from radio, television, and the movies). However, I had only the vaguest conception of what a university administrator might do or be. Until I read the Claremont announcement, I had given little thought to the possibility of university administration in my future. The life of the full-time faculty member is sweet (or perhaps it only appears so in retrospect). Even the student protests that shook university campuses during the seventies were intellectually exhilarating since they challenged us, the faculty to defend not only our research paradigms, but our very conception of knowledge. However, the Claremont announcement did capture my attention, so I suppose that somewhere in the nether regions of my mind, I was nurturing a thought that at some point I might be interested in becoming dean of a School of Social Work. Or perhaps student unrest had raised even more fundamental questions about the mission of the university in times of enormous social transformations—questions which could best be addressed from an administrative position. In any event, I submitted my letter of application.

The letter of rejection I received a few weeks later was devastating because it was so unexpected. Up until that point, my education and my career had been filled with positive experiences, although within circumscribed environments, that is, undergraduate studies in a historically black university, graduate studies in a School of Social Work (one of the least hostile environments in academic communities for students of color), and employment in public-sector agencies. Once a staff person at the regional office of the Fulbright program in Houston had discouraged me when I had stopped in to request an application because, according to her, the program was "highly competitive." As I left the office with application materials that I had practically wrestled from her, I forgave her lack of faith in my competitive ability; after all, I theorized, she had not bothered to ask a single question about my education or experience; she had not bothered to find out that I had graduated Magna Cum Laude and Phi Beta Kappa from Howard and had earned the M.S.W. from UC Berkeley before I was twenty-one and two years later was a field instructor for the School of Social Work at the University of Texas. She only saw a young black woman who, from her perspective, had little chance of competing with all those white applicants from Yale, Princeton, Vassar, Michigan, and Stanford. Perhaps if I had followed through and applied for the Fulbright, I might have discovered that she was right, but I decided to get married instead, and we moved from Houston to Los Angeles.

Without much experience with rejection, the Claremont letter was particularly bitter to receive, and I could not let the board's decision go unchallenged. I telephoned the project director at Claremont who had signed the letter of rejection. I indicated that the letter had not been very informative and I would appreciate hearing directly why my application had not been considered favorably by the selection committee. I was told that my application had revealed that I was already in a position to succeed in a university since I had already been promoted and received tenure. The program had been designed for women who had not had my opportunities. It was designed to give women access to administrative positions that otherwise might not be forthcoming. The implication was that a minority female who had already achieved more than could have been expected—a tenured position in a major research university—was less likely to find impediments to upward mobility, and therefore the program would not provide "added value."

I have no way of knowing whether any white women also were rejected for the same reason; however, even if one or more were, I would still consider this reasoning when applied to African American applicants as institutional racism, particularly if it were the determining factor in whether the applicant was accepted or rejected. It was not an example of an act of discrimination on the part of project staff, but rather an example of a policy which would have the same effect. The policy to exclude all faculty who had achieved tenure would assume that in the struggle for upward mobility, a white female with tenure and a black female with tenure are advantaged to the same degree when compared to their untenured sisters. Since it could be demonstrated that at that time, in the 1970s, race was a greater obstacle to upward mobility than gender, this equal application of the policy to black and white female applicants could be considered an example of institutional racism.

Americans who are members of racial minority groups and white Americans often mean different things when using the same terms. Reporting on a study conducted at the University of California at Berkeley, Troy Duster, an African American sociologist, pointed out that minority students and white students meant different things when they identified indicators of "commitment to diversity." The white students considered it to mean a willingness to associate with those of different ethnic groups, to "party" with them, to share beer and pizza. To most minority students, however, a "commitment to diversity" meant support for affirmative action in admissions or faculty recruitment. Similarly, minority and majority faculty may mean different things when using the term *racism*. For majority members, racism more frequently means the direct expression of hostility toward or lack of respect for an individual based on his or her race or ethnicity. For minority faculty, racism more frequently means not only the direct expression of these attitudes but the passive acceptance of policies and procedures which result in inequities more often for minorities than for nonminorities.

The concept of racism as institutional rather than individual has been clearly defined in the social science literature. In my academic career in a predominantly white institution, it is the institutional form which I have most frequently encountered. The difference between those minority faculty who "succeed" (i.e., get tenure, move into senior administrative posts) and those who do not may well be their ability to overcome the effects of institutional racism.

After I was not accepted in the Claremont program, I spent that sabbatical year writing a book which was undoubtedly a major factor in my promotion to full professor two years later. A graduate student from South Africa who had taught in a school of social work in South Africa reported to me that the book had been used in her classes despite the fact that it had been banned by the South African government. I considered this the ultimate compliment! The Claremont experience behind me, I totally committed to teaching and research and I no longer thought seriously about administration. Was it because I now believed that my earlier interest was misguided or was it an overreaction to the experience of rejection? If I had continued to pursue an interest in administration, would I have experienced few obstacles as the selection committee at Claremont assumed or would I have needed, as I had assumed, a program like the one at Claremont to compensate for the disadvantage imposed by being black as well as female? It is difficult to settle on answers to these questions.

In 1978, Kanter, Wheatley, and associates distributed their evaluation of five training programs funded by the Carnegie Corporation of New York and conducted during the 1970s, one of which was the Women in Administration program at Claremont. The evaluators concluded that the programs had had limited effect on upward mobility of participants since career success seems to come not from training but rather from the positions people hold.

I suppose that on the basis of this evaluation, I did not suffer any great loss by not being accepted into the Claremont program. However, it should also be pointed out that evaluation of such programs conducted a decade earlier leads to assessments that followed too closely on the heels of the training programs to permit an accurate gauge of longer term career advancement. Thus the relevance of the findings for training opportunities was circumscribed.

If a training program is not an effective mechanism for developing administrative skills and significantly improving one's chances at upward mobility, it may be an effective mechanism for increasing our understanding of the ways in which race or ethnicity acts to expedite or depress upward mobility. The need for this understanding may not have been as evident in the 1970s as it is now in the 1990s. Again, in my own case, there have been specific experiences which suggest that my race has had and will continue to have both positive and negative effects on my upward mobility.

Accentuating the Positive

There has been more written about the negative effects of race or ethnicity on access to senior administrative positions in higher education than about positive effects. Institutional racism is encountered as frequently as soul music or barbecued ribs in the daily lives of every African American, including those who have overcome the odds to become senior administrators in prestigious universities. However, despite the disadvantages, it cannot be denied that there are also sometimes advantages to being a minority.

I am convinced that the fact that I was an African American faculty member in a major research university may have been taken into account when in 1986 I was selected as one of the "Faculty Who Make a Difference" to be honored at the annual meeting of the American Association of Higher Education in Washington, D.C. I am also fairly certain that the visibility this earned for me on my own campus was a factor when later that year the provost at USC was considering candidates for the position of acting dean of graduate studies. The incumbent in that position had been asked to take a temporary position as dean of the College of Letters, Arts, and Sciences, and it was not clear whether he would or would not accept it later on a permanent basis. Visibility and being in the right place at the right time have been identified as significant factors in upward mobility in higher education administration. In some measure, minority status guarantees high visibility.

The fact that I was part of an underrepresented minority group actually may have counterbalanced other factors which mitigated against my selection as graduate dean. On the one hand, the overwhelming majority of academic leaders are drawn from the faculty and some academicians feel that an acceptable career pattern is merely to fall into administration, learn on the job, and then be called to the next level of responsibility by virtue of having done reasonably well in the position that one is vacating. However, the pathways that lead from faculty to administrative positions are broader and more clearly defined if one is a faculty member in some disciplines as compared to others.

The senior administrator of an academic will almost invariably will have a terminal degree in that discipline (e.g., the chair of the English Deptartment will have a Ph.D. in English, etc.). Although sizeable numbers of persons get doctorates in a School of Education with a specialization in "Higher Education," the vast majority of senior administrators in the arts and sciences (deans or associate deans in the Colleges of Arts and Sciences, vice presidents for academic affairs, or dean of graduate studies, etc.) have degrees in an academic rather than a professional discipline. There is a general sense that an attitudinal indicator of the disregard of academicians for the field of higher education management can be seen in the relatively low prestige enjoyed by the discipline of education and by the accepted tradition that the Ed.D. and Ph.D. in education are generally not the most desirable credentials for academic administrators in four-year institutions. Until my appointment as dean of graduate studies, there had been no graduate dean in any major university from the discipline of social work.

The majority of the Ph.D. programs for which the dean of graduate studies is administratively responsible are in the arts and sciences, and it is therefore almost always a faculty member from the arts and sciences who becomes graduate dean. The provost was able to rationalize my appointment—despite the fact that my discipline is social work—because (1) social work is one of the disciplines in the university in which the Ph.D is awarded; (2) I had administrative experience as director of the Social Work Research Center (although only part-time); and (3) the appointment was only "acting," so that if, for some reason, I was found to be unacceptable by my colleagues, I could easily return to the faculty and the School of Social Work. Nevertheless, perhaps more compelling than all of these reasons was the fact that there were no minority senior administrators in the university—not on the twenty-two-member Council of Deans or among the six vice presidents.

Affirmative action is supposed to insure that competent minority persons are considered despite the fact that they might not be present in the usual pools from which applicants are solicited. There is general agreement about the particular competencies of effective academic administrators, although assessing the competence is often far from objective. For example, it is clear that the skills to be honed are not the same as those of the teacher and researcher and are rarely related to any specific discipline. Academic officers not only are intellectual leaders who shape the curriculum and translate the institutional mission into a meaningful educational program, but they are also budget officers, long-range planners, and personnel specialists.

It is part of the accepted belief system in most major universities that the qualities needed to be an effective administrator can be learned if one has demonstrated one's ability to perform the primary research and teaching functions of the university and have been confirmed by one's peers through the promotion and tenure process. One should be capable of learning to elicit a collective vision, to negotiate among the varied constituencies in order to build coalitions and consensus; to integrate relevant information about financial aid, admissions, public relations; and to understand the implications of changing social, political, and technological forces as they affect the institution in the short range and in the long range.

Despite the rhetoric of affirmative action, these beliefs do not always extend to minorities. Frequently, minorities are considered to be less likely to have the necessary qualities not due, as would probably be pointed out, to any less intelligence, motivation, or energy, but because they are less likely to have had the appointments presumed to be necessary in order for the necessary learning to take place. It is ironic that certain mindsets about career paths prevail in spite of ample evidence that only some chairs become deans and few deans become presidents. Yet, the fact that a minority candidate has never been a chair can effectively preclude consideration for the position of dean, and the fact that the minority candidate has never served as dean may effectively preclude consideration for the position of president.

Affirmative action may be ineffective for reasons less consequential than a candidate's presumed inexperience. As a member of a search committee for the presidency of the university, I remember the remark made by one of the members reporting on his interview with a particular candidate: "He looks presidential." I was left quite certain that anyone dark-skinned, short, or female did not have "the look."

The Advantage of Having Access to Networks

The push to increase the number of underrepresented minorities in higher education has virtually assured that a minority faculty member who has successfully climbed the promotion and tenure ladder will be identified, recruited, and offered access to a number of key roles in associations dealing with higher education. Three months after I became acting dean of graduate studies at the University of Southern California, I received an invitation to attend a forum sponsored by the American Council on Education (ACE). In 1977, ACE established the National Identification Program for the Advancement of Women in Higher Education. An important component of this program is a series of meetings to which approximately twenty women who have been identified as "emerging and established leaders" in higher education administration are invited. The agenda at the meetings included an exploration of factors associated with upward mobility in institutions of higher education from interviews with search committees to the negotiation of campus politics. Perhaps the most important aspect, however, was the inclusion of participants in a network which is a primary source of female candidates for senior administrators (presidents, vice presidents, and deans). In 1980 a special focus on minority women was incorporated into the program in order to increase the probability that minority women would be recruited and promoted. The swiftness of the invitation to me was undoubtedly due to this particular concern about the inclusion of minority women. I can attest to the fact that participation in the ACE forum not only increased my understanding of key issues confronting universities in our society, but also sharpened my awareness that the skills and competencies for being an effective administrator were in my grasp.

The fact that I am a minority senior administrator in a major research university has also contributed to the number and nature of other opportunities made available to me. I have chaired the Board of Directors of the Council of Graduate Schools and served on its Executive Committee. I have served on the Executive Committees of the Association of Graduate Schools and the Graduate Record Examination Board. I have also chaired the Minority Graduate Education Committee of the GRE Board The fact of the matter is that if I were to join any organization that deals with higher education, I would more than likely also be called upon to serve on its board and committees. I would like to believe that it is solely because of my outstanding qualifications, but I am realistic enough to know that status as an underrepresented minority in almost all of these organizations inevitably enhances my eligibility for leadership positions.

Acknowledging the Negative

A great deal has been written about the disadvantages of being a minority person in higher education especially if one aspires to a senior administrative position. However, I generally tend to be, if not exactly a Pollyanna, a believer in the basic goodness of man (and woman!) and that many, if not most, of the negative experiences I have encountered are a consequence of my own actions, attitudes, or beliefs. Thus, if I choose not to seek a higher position when the opportunity arises to do so, it must be my own lack of ambition rather than any external influences. If I am perceived as less competent than others, I have clearly failed to communicate the knowledge and skills that I possess; or if I am overwhelmed with obligations that have little to do with my primary job description, then perhaps I need to go into therapy in order to find out why I have so much difficulty in saying, "No!" However, there is evidence to support the notion that some of the problems encountered by minority faculty and administrators in institutions of higher education are not due to personal deficiencies but rather to the fact that they are members of an ethnic minority group.

The Problem of Depressed Aspirations

I have suggested that the most serious outcome of my rejection for the Claremont Women in Administration program was a shutdown on my emerging interest in administration. On the one hand, since the program was explicitly for women, the rejection was more clearly related to the perception that an overprepared, highly qualified woman with a proven record of accomplishment essentially "has it made." On the other hand, the fact was overlooked that minority women—even those who are overprepared, highly qualified, and have proven records of accomplishment may not have the same access as nonminority women to the role models, the good contacts, and the sponsorship that can make the difference between self-doubt and self-confidence, between healthy ambition and depressed aspirations. Approximately five years after that sabbatical year the opportunity arose for me to consider the position of dean of the School of Social Work in my own institution. After the incumbent dean (who had been my dissertation chair) announced his intent to step down at the end of the year, the faculty voted unanimously for an internal promotion rather than a national search for the new dean. A search committee was formed, and its first act was to send a memo to all faculty inviting them to nominate anyone on the faculty who in their opinion should be considered for the position. Five names were submitted, and each nominee was then interviewed by a member of the search committee to determine their interest. When I was interviewed, I made it clear that I had no interest.

A faculty member's disinterest in or even disdain for administration is a common enough attitude, and many professors fear that they may become infected with a managerial mentality. Therefore, in both small and large ways, faculty make clear that endowed chairs, distinguished lectures, interdisciplinary symposia, new and "state of the art" laboratory equipment, new library holdings, and major research grants are all more important than administrative offices, the president's house, or staff retreats. Similarly, the decision to teach and do research is most often attributed to a desire for intellectual stimulation, but the choice to administer is most often associated with a desire for money, power, or status. Administrators who come from the faculty and still hold a faculty appointment frequently point this out. More than one university president has even expressed the opinion that although they have not been in the classroom on a regular basis for ten years or so, they have yearned at times to return.

Perhaps the only reason to question my decision not to permit my name to be brought forward in consideration for the deanship of the School of Social Work in 1980 is the fact that five or six years earlier, I had been interested enough to consider spending a sabbatical year increasing administrative knowledge and skills. The intensive immersion in the Women in Administration program with an opportunity to gain confidence in my ability to master the required skills might have been enough to counterbalance the intense gratification received from teaching and research. If the program had included exposure to other minority colleagues who had made the transition from faculty to senior administrator or exposure to a senior administrator of any race or ethnicity who would provide encouragement for my aspirations, I might not have been so quick to refuse to be considered for the position or for the dozen or so other deanships for which I was recruited.

The Problem of Negative Stereotyping

There have been noticeable changes in the relationships between deans and faculty members over the last three decades. As colleges and universities have adopted a "corporate" style of administration, deans are now as likely to be seen as managers, rather than colleagues. Graduate deans occupy an unusual place within their institutions because they have no control over, and only occasional direct contact with faculty members except in committee meetings and task forces. Still, they have responsibility for ensuring quality instruction at the highest degree level.

The authority of the graduate dean although limited can have painful consequences when exerted. For example, students may be denied admission if they do not meet standards set by the graduate school even if the department recommends their admission. Qualifying examination committees can be told that their procedures were unfair and be required to re-examine a student. A faculty member who has not been involved actively in his or her own research may not be approved to chair doctoral research committees. The graduate dean is often the final arbiter in conflicts between faculty and students or even between faculty and faculty. If the graduate dean is a minority member and the faculty or graduate student has been unaccustomed to minorities in roles of authority, the result often can be an abrasive encounter.

An engineering faculty member, Professor X, was incensed when I denied his petition for a student who had been newly admitted to the Ph.D. program in the fall semester to take his qualifying examination early in the spring semester of the same academic year. Graduate School policy required that students complete at least twenty-four units of course work prior to taking the qualifying examination. This professor was anxious to have the student begin his doctoral research on a project in his laboratory and, therefore, wanted to have the qualifying examination expedited. At the time of the professor's request, the student had not completed a single semester in the program. This did not keep Professor X from accusing me of being "rigid" in my refusal to waive policy. Moreover, he suggested, "If you had supervised doctoral students, you would know that some are prepared earlier than others to take the qualifying examination and should be accommodated."

I was stunned that he assumed that I was inexperienced in the supervision of doctoral research despite the fact that I had chaired or been a member of more than fifty dissertation committees over a period of more than twenty years! Professor X had been a faculty member for more than ten years during which two other graduate deans had served. My predecessors had been highly respected scholars—in electrical engineering and biological sciences. They were also white and male. I could only believe that Professor X had assumed that my ascension to the deanship had been an "affirmative action" appointment and that I did not have the same qualifications and therefore the competence to match that of the former deans.

The Problem of Extra Burdens

It is, of course, demeaning to minority faculty or administrators to have nonminority colleagues assume that they are not as competent. The irony is that, in many instances, minority faculty are required to have greater knowledge and minority administrators are required to have broader skills than these peers. As a minority faculty member, I was often asked to serve as "outside member" on dissertation committees in departments only remotely related to my own when the research topic embraced some aspect of minority culture or issues. The rationale for the invitation to serve was the fact that the department had no minority faculty who could provide a certain perspective on the student's research.

As dean of graduate studies, I had administrative responsibility for all the Ph.D. programs in the university and oversight responsibility for all of the graduate and professional degree programs. However, as a minority graduate dean, I was called upon to take a leadership role in activities that scarcely can be associated with graduate education. For example, I chaired the advisory committee to USC's Academic Initiative in the Neighborhood, an educational enhancement program that targets minority junior and eventually senior high school students. It has only a minimal relationship to postbaccalaureate programs in the university. Yet I was involved for nearly two years in active efforts to develop the program. It developed out of consideration for the need for an intensive, creative program to recruit minority students as undergraduates to the university. It was concluded that most such efforts in the past had been aimed at accessing a finite and limited pool of students, but few activities had been aimed at increasing the pool.

Our university is located in the midst of a minority-rich inner-city neighborhood in which the drop-out rate of students from local high schools is the highest in the city. It appears unconscionable to compete with every other university in our efforts to recruit minority students from all over the United States when we have done nothing to increase the number of minority students who graduate from high schools in our own community and who are eligible for admission. The university's best opportunity to increase dramatically its minority student population at both graduate and undergraduate levels would be to develop a program aimed at increasing the pool. It was also clear that if the university were to move in that direction it would require the "hands-on" leadership of a senior administrator who was knowledgeable about education in the inner city and deeply committed to the development of a university-based initiative to make a difference. At its inception, I was the single person in that category.

Anticipating the Future

The social and cultural changes that have taken place in the last century have accelerated rapidly so that in a single lifetime, a person can experience successive waves of change which are usually progressive in nature. As a consequence, many African Americans, including academics, are subject to what might be called a "regret syndrome." We see opportunities which we never had now available to persons who are only a few years behind us. It is perhaps the same experience as that of the outstanding baseball players who played in the old Negro League prior to the desegregation of professional baseball. They must have wondered how much they could have achieved if they had had the same opportunity as Jackie Robinson or Roy Campanella or Hank Aaron to play in the major leagues. There are also African American Ph.D.s who were already fifty years old in 1970 and therefore past the outer limits of the eligible pool of minority scholars who could take advantage of the affirmative action surge that began then. We cannot discount the possibility that there are now retired African American faculty who are keenly aware that if they had come along twenty years later, they might have had the mentoring that would have facilitated access to research funding and enhanced publication opportunities and consequently prepared them to be considered favorably for positions such as provost or president in a major research university.

There is also concern about what lies ahead. There is the progress we still have to make so that there are the same opportunities for minorities to leave senior administrative posts in universities at the vice president or president level and become directors of major foundations or associations in higher education.

Obvious differences also still exist in the opportunities available for those minorities who wish to stay in university administration and use their training and experiences to move into bigger, more complex institutions, as compared to their white counterparts. It is not uncommon to see whites who serve as CEOs of two, three or even four institutions or systems of higher education during their careers. All the while, qualified minority candidates sit and wait for an opportunity.

African Americans in almost any field of endeavor often sense that there is information or unstated "rules of the game" which influence their ability to perform their jobs effectively or to have a chance at upward mobility. Sometimes, it is not clear whether some positions are "up" or "down." For example, if one moves from dean of a School of Business or Law or Education to vice president for minority affairs, is that a real promotion? Where does a dean go after the "deaning" is over?

There are two primary perceptions of the position of academic dean. One is that "deaning" is essentially a "time out" from the primary work of the institution:

> This perspective is rooted in the traditional view of the academy as an environment that is dedicated to the life of the mind. Serving as a dean is a job that someone has to do—the institution does have certain administrative functions that have to be taken care of. But after one has done his or her duty in the deanship, the reward is the return to the ranks of the faculty.

The exception to this scenario is the instance when the challenges and rewards of administration have become so seductive that the dean now aspires to even greater challenges such as those encountered as provost or vice president for academic affairs or as president of the university. However, even in these instances, the mythology is that tenancy is only temporary and retirement will most likely be preceded by a return to the full-time faculty. The conventional attitude is that even a president should welcome one last fling at the good life of the scholar.

Whether a dean chooses to return to the faculty or to seek other challenges would appear to be purely a matter of personal preference. A dean's access to opportunities for upward mobility should be provided solely on the basis of competency. However, as an African American whose entire academic career has been spent at a predominantly white research university, I am aware that other factors often intrude, and for minorities, some of these factors are related to minority status. For example, if there are no other minority administrators and, therefore, no other role models for minority faculty and students, a sense of obligation may outweigh a preference to return to the classroom or research laboratory. However, opportunities to become a provost or president—at least in a smaller or less prestigious institution—will probably be expanded for minority faculty or administrators who have achieved some national visibility.

It might be suggested that my career has been exceptional in many respects. The three years it took me to complete my doctorate in social work was unusually short. The average time was approximately five years in 1966, although the average has been increasing just as it has for the Ph.D. in arts and science disciplines. The three years to tenure was also exceptional, although in the early seventies more faculty were given tenure prior to the six- year maximum that is more customary today. Neither females nor African Americans of either gender are likely to be found as directors of research institutes in major research universities or deans of graduate schools. Apparently, racism has not been an effective brake on my career mobility.

As indicated earlier, the goal of exploratory studies, including the case study, is not to test hypotheses but to generate hypotheses. On the basis of this exploration of a single and unorthodox career pathway, several questions have emerged as deserving of more rigorous empirical investigation. For example, are African American faculty more likely to advance to administrative careers in their own institution than in a different institution? Are African Americans in senior academic positions (dean, vice president of academic affairs, president) more likely to have doctorates in education than whites who hold those positions? Are there significant differences in the career pathways of white women, African American women, and other minority women? To what extent do "extra burdens" influence upward mobility for African American faculty? Are there significant differences in the options available to minority and nonminority administrators at the end of tenure? Are there significant differences in the choices made by African American administrators and other administrators in regard to their career or the end of tenure?

Tentative answers to these and other questions suggested by case studies in this book may be stated as hypotheses and tested in future research. The findings from such research may help to increase our sensitivity to the opportunities as well as the obstacles for African Americans and other minorities seeking careers in higher education administration. If another Women in Administration program is conducted in the next decade with similar objectives to the Claremont program of the seventies, I would expect that there would be heightened sensitivity to the particular disadvantage of African American women in institutions of higher education whose issues are not identical to those of their white sisters. The measure of that sensitivity will include the extent to which eligibility for the program takes into consideration factors other than the applicant's education and experience such as the extent to which it recognizes that skill in overcoming the consequences of institutional racism will need to be developed. These skills can be learned in the same way that one learns to overcome any other conflict between the individual and the social order.

CHAPTER 9

Observations and Intuitions

WILLIAM B. HARVEY

No Crystal Staircase

The wide variety of circumstances, situations, incidents, and encounters that any person may experience in life makes it difficult, if not impossible, to determine who will emerge to lead important social institutions. It could be argued that the determinant of leadership is as much biological as it is environmental, which validates the perspective that some people are born to greatness, while others have it thrust upon them. Whatever the considerations that cause leaders to move to the front of the pack ahead of their peers and into decision-making positions, there is much to be gained from having these special individuals share with the rest of us the ways in which they have been able to realize their personal and professional development.

In contributing their commentaries to this volume, the men and women who are included here have scaled the ladders of administrative success in the various colleges and universities where they have worked. Their observations remind us—in no uncertain terms—that even in the ivory tower of academe, racism and prejudice live on. They contend that even in the intellectual arena, there is still no level playing field for African Americans. This acknowledgment will not sit well with some people who operate within these environs nor with their supporters, champions, and protectors in boardrooms, legislative chambers, media studios, and elsewhere; but objective, reasonable, and fair-minded readers will recognize the truth and poignancy of these messages. These essays convey pain and struggle, but they also deliver hope and optimism; they transmit frustration and anger, but they also present forgiveness and understanding. Through their collective experiences, the authors identify several individual and institutional phenomena operating in colleges and universities that merit further scrutiny.

Of the eight contributors to this volume, six are alumni of historically black colleges and universities, and each of these individuals attributes the academic and personal growth experiences that they received in these institutions as being significant factors in their development and maturation. They speak clearly and loudly of the high expectations that were placed upon them and of the nurturing individuals and supportive climates that helped prepare them to meet the challenges that were put before them. These observations stand in stark contrast to the two contributors who attended predominantly white institutions, both of whom exited from their undergraduate alma maters with feelings of dissatisfaction, if not rancor. While recognizing that the physical facilities at their institutions of choice were less well developed than they would have liked, each of the HBCU graduates felt well prepared from both cognitive and affective standpoints as they entered graduate school and found themselves in competition with white students from all over the country. Although most of the contributors entered college at a time when the majority of African American students attended HBCUs, the positive nature of their experiences is worth noting.

Each author pays homage to others who have provided assistance to him or her through the various stages of his or her career. In several of the commentaries, the networking, role models, and mentoring were identified as being significant. Each contributor shares experiences of encounters with racism and relates the way in which he or she responded to the situation, or declined to respond. The recollections of situations that occurred during the authors' childhoods as they tried to make personal adjustments to a racially segregated society may stir uncomfortable feelings, but the sentiments can be attributed to an era that has long since passed. However, the indignities that occurred after the authors had achieved some recognition and standing in the higher education community, cannot be dismissed so easily. They point to an undercurrent of racial prejudice that, from time to time, bubbles up to the surface and debunks the myth that colleges and universities are different in kind or degree from other institutional structures.

For those who have never suffered its bite, it may be difficult to comprehend the psychological anguish that is caused by racism. Though we would sometimes rather not confront the reality of the situation, this perverse attitude is so deeply embedded in the American fabric, that even for African Americans who have achieved success and recognition, there is the realization that at any second, an incident or an utterance can occur that penetrates one's aura of worth and diminishes one's sense of self. Some successful African Americans choose not to dwell on painful and bitter past experiences, let alone share them in a public fashion, and this approach is entirely understandable. It has even become fashionable in certain circles lately for some African Americans who have reached a certain level of accomplishment to deny or diminish the effects of racism and, in some extreme cases, even its very existence. This is precisely why it is the honest presentation of this ugly manifestation of the underside of the American character that will do the most to move it into the graveyard of aberrant behavior where it belongs. Having successful, intelligent, talented African Americans, such as the contributors to this volume, detail the ways in which they overcame racism should help all of us to consider how we too can attack the monster and put its misery out of us.

One of the issues that is touched upon in this volume that has great significance as we move into the new millennium is the relationship between African Americans and Hispanics on college and university campuses. Both groups remain substantially underrepresented in practically every category of students and academic professionals, and with the political and the institutional movement away from affirmative action in many states, these two minority constituencies could find themselves unwittingly pitted against one another. It would be advantageous for African American and Hispanic academicians to enter into alliances around common concerns and issues, rather than compete with one another against an institutional power structure that has historically excluded members of both groups from having appropriate representation, let alone positions of power and authority. Demographic analyses project that, relative to those of whites, increases in the percentages of the total population will occur in both the African American and Hispanic communities over the next two decades because of higher birth rates and immigration trends. The necessity to have colleges and universities reflect the needs and concerns of these communities in their curricula, teaching cadre, and administrative staff, and in their student populations as well, is greater now than it has been at any time in the nation's history. Given the glacial pace of change in higher education, it seems not only advisable, but necessary, for African American and Hispanic scholars and administrators to sit down and strategize together about ways in which they can use whatever collective social, economic, and political influences they can muster to modify institutional behavior in ways that will benefit their respective communities.

Institutions of higher education in which African Americans and Hispanics are represented in significant percentages within the overall population will be places for the greatest opportunity for mutual involvement, and at the same time, they can conceivably become places where the greatest level of friction between the two groups can also occur. A paucity of senior-level administrative and faculty representatives from these groups does not necessarily mean that a given institution will not be as responsive to concerns about diversity as it might be, but many institutions simply pay lip service to the cause while they do nothing to modify either the climate or the patterns of behavior that cause this situation to occur. The times and circumstances in which we live call for a proactive strategy to induce desired change, and while it may be more comfortable to wait to be approached, African Americans can initiate contact with their Hispanic colleagues, or vice versa, to find ways in which they can work with each other to increase the level of receptivity and representation of both groups in the institutions where they feel unwelcome and underrepresented.

Idiosyncracies and Constants

Advertisements for senior-level administrative positions frequently will contain a statement that indicates that the salary is to be paid commensurate with the qualifications and experiences of the successful candidate. There is often a wide variance in salary among administrators who may appear to have similar degrees of institutional responsibility. No substantive studies are known to exist in which race is a significant consideration in payment of different salary levels to senior administrative persons. At the dean's level, the general rule is that medical, business, and sometimes law school deans tend to be among the highest paid persons who hold that job title, while at the lower end are frequently deans of library science, social work, and education. Vice presidents of academic affairs are often the highest paid persons at that level of administration, with student affairs vice presidents usually found at the lower end. Presidential salaries will vary, with the size and type of the institution being the significant considerations.

It is noteworthy that, for the majority of contributors to this volume, salary issues were not identified as being significant problems as they accepted their various appointments over the years. In the one case where there was an obvious and significant discrepancy in the salary that the person was offered and accepted, compared to his colleagues, the issue was resolved without prolonged wrangling in the next salary adjustment process. The contributors were also largely silent on the issue of regular salary increases, so one might assume that they did not experience what they considered to be unfair or inappropriate treatment in that area.

A factor that is closer to home, so to speak, is the significance of the families of the contributors in the individual realization of success. No definitive or precise pattern can be seen to emerge from these cases. While some persons relied heavily on their family members for strength and support, others did not identify their families as playing a disproportionate role in their movement upward to a top administrative position. This observation is not intended to suggest that family support was not present and appreciated in each situation, but simply to note that the acknowledgment of such support was given greater mention by some individuals than by others. In situations such as those presented in this volume, where racism would amplify the stress that accompanies movement up the administrative ladder, there may be some instances in which the circumstances related to upward mobility caused some damage to family relationships. Certainly, this would not be a surprising outcome in scenarios as complex as those presented by these commentators.

Contrary to what might be considered as the prevailing wisdom, which suggests that the route to top administrative positions is defined by certain appropriate academic backgrounds and pathways, several of the contributors to this volume earned their degrees in education—a field which has not been a fertile area for those who hold senior-level appointments in predominantly white colleges and universities. Further, not all of them moved through the professorial ranks prior to securing their administrative posts. The historical perspective has been that individuals who move to the vice presidential level and higher generally have earned Ph.D.s in an area from the liberal arts and sciences, rather than from a professional school, such as education, social work, or nursing. However, top-level administrators have more frequently had backgrounds from other professional schools, such as medicine, engineering, and, particularly, law.

Three of the contributors to this volume, two who have reached the presidential level and the other who held a vice presidency, have their graduate preparation in the field of education. In only a few cases are references to their academic area of expertise made by the contributors, which would suggest that they did not experience any consistent negative response to this situation as their administrative careers unfolded. One contributor notes that, for him, holding a doctorate in a nontraditional academic field is only one of the areas in which he deviated from the status quo, since he had also never been a full-time faculty member and since he had moved into top-level academic affairs administration from a student affairs position. His path would be considered unusual in several respects, although there are other members of this group who while they sometimes taught, did not hold faculty status on a consistent basis.

The fact is that a disproportionate number of African Americans who hold doctoral degrees have received them in education, and when they hold administrative appointments in predominantly white institutions, they tend to be more concentrated in student affairs than in other areas. Thus the achievements and positions that have been realized by the cohort of administrators whose stories have been presented in this volume may signal that some of the walls of tradition that have restricted advancement in academic administration are beginning to come down. In some sense, the old patterns still proved effective for five contributors, meaning that each of them moved up the academic ladder as faculty members. Four of the contributors received their academic training in the sciences, which certainly has been a "safe" and acceptable area from which to proceed into academic administration, while the other person holds degrees in social work, another of the nontraditional fields.

One bothersome situation that seemed to plague several of the contributors was the resistance or insubordination that they experienced from individuals who held positions that were below theirs. In both overt and covert ways, certain people at some of the institutions represented here worked, behaved, and acted in ways that one does not expect to occur within the context of relationships in which one person holds a higher position than the other. Sometimes the actions were tacit, such as questioning the judgment or decisions of the African American administrator; in other cases they were more direct, such as refusing to carry out an action that had been requested or withholding certain items that would be expected to be provided without hesitation or challenge. As noted, predominantly white colleges and universities have been by design, until quite recently, institutions where whites have exercised a monopoly on positions of power, and the incidents that are characterized in this volume indicate that there are still people on the campuses, at various levels in the institutional hierarchies, who have difficulty accepting and responding to an African American in a high-level administrative post. In several cases, the degree of support that the authors received from their peer administrators was also disappointing, and there were a number of situations in which high levels of racial insensitivity were displayed by college and university officials. To the degree that the campus climate is set, or at least significantly influenced by the actions, interactions, and communications of the top-level administrators, some of the incidents that have been presented in this volume suggest that there may be less proactive effort on this front than is desirable from those key individuals in order to facilitate an environment that is intentionally welcoming and encouraging to African Americans and members of other minority groups.

The defining characteristic among the individuals whose stories have been presented here is that they are all deeply anxious that others be able to follow in the paths that they have trod. There is a clear sense of concern and caring for the well-being of the African American community, and especially for the young people who are now making their way through colleges and universities like the ones where the contributors have served. Though none of the authors makes the statement in quite this way, the message that resonates throughout these writings is, "No one else should have to go through the things that I did—just because they are African American—to advance to a position like the one I hold." It would be ideal if that sentiment were realized, but only the most committed optimist would suggest that it is likely to occur any time in the near future without some stringent changes in attitudes and behavior. At this very minute, some of the same kinds of distressing incidents that were faced by the contributors to this volume are likely to be occurring on a college or university campus. Not nearly enough has been done to confront the existence of racism, let alone purge it from our institutions of higher learning, and this is a challenge that all members of the academic community should join forces to meet, with vigor and zest.

It is important to realize that there are compelling economic, political, social, and moral reasons for making the society less fixated with skin color and more focused on capabilities and possibilities. The presence of people on college and university campuses like those who have offered their commentaries in this volume would prompt us to hope that they will impact their institutions in a way that the perspectives of their administrative and faculty colleagues will be broadened, as will the range of learning experiences that will be provided to the student population. More than ever before, institutions of higher education have become the places that prepare the future leaders to carry out their responsibilities to those whom they will lead. As the leaders of the next generation move into, through, and out of the classrooms, laboratories, and libraries of our colleges and universities, it is important that we strive to see that whatever their roots may be, they grow and develop to the fullest extent of their capabilities, with no ceilings or limits imposed on them because of their racial heritage. The commentaries that have been collected here offer us a sprinkling of the ultimate possibilities.

List of Contributors

Althia deGraft-Johnson is former Vice President for Academic Affairs at United States International University, San Diego.

Vera Ferris is President of Richard Stockton College, Pomona, NJ.

Wesley Harris is Professor of Aeronautics and Astronautics at the Massachusetts Institute of Technology.

William B. Harvey is Dean of the School of Education at the University of Wisconsin-Milwaukee.

Horace Judson is President of the State University of New York at Plattsburgh.

Reatha Clark King is President and Executive Director of The General Mills Foundation and Former President of Metropolitan State University, MN.

Marie McDemmond is President of Norfolk State University (Va.)

Charlie Nelms is Chancellor Emeritus of the University of Michigan-Flint and former Chancellor of Indiana University-East. His current position is Vice President for Student Services and Diversity at Indiana University.

Barbara Solomon is Vice Provost for Minority Affairs and former Dean of the Graduate School at the University of Southern California.

Index

SUNY series: Frontiers in Education
Philip G. Altbach, Editor

List of Titles

Class, Race, and Gender in American Education—Lois Weis (ed.)

Excellence and Equality: A Qualitatively Different Perspective on Gifted and Talented Education—David M. Fetterman

Change and Effectiveness in Schools: A Cultural Perspective—Gretchen B. Rossman, H. Dickson Corbett, and William A. Firestone

The Curriculum: Problems, Politics, and Possibilities—Landon E. Beyer and Michael W. Apple (eds.)

The Character of American Higher Education and Intercollegiate Sports—Donald Chu

Crisis in Teaching: Perspectives on Current Reforms—Lois Weis, Philip G. Altbach, Gail P. Kelly, Hugh G. Petrie, and Sheila Slaughter (eds.)

The High Status Track: Studies of Elite Schools and Stratification—Paul William Kingston and Lionel S. Lewis (eds.)

The Economics of American Universities: Management, Operations, and Fiscal Environment—Stephen A. Hoenack and Eileen L. Collins (eds.)

The Higher Learning and High Technology: Dynamics of Higher Education and Policy Formation—Sheila Slaughter

Dropouts from Schools: Issues, Dilemmas and Solutions—Lois Weis, Eleanor Farrar, and Hugh G. Petrie (eds.)

Religious Fundamentalism and American Education: The Battle for the Public Schools—Eugene F. Provenzo, Jr.

Going to School: The African-American Experience—Kofi Lomotey (ed.)

Curriculum Differentiation: Interpretive Studies in U.S. Secondary Schools—Reba Page and Linda Valli (eds.)

The Racial Crisis in American Higher Education—Philip G. Altbach and Kofi Lomotey (eds.)

The Great Transformation in Higher Education, 1960–1980—Clark Kerr

College in Black and White: African-American Students in Predominantly White and in Historically Black Public Universities—Walter R. Allen, Edgar G. Epps, and Nesha Z. Haniff (eds.)

Textbooks in American Society: Politics, Policy, and Pedagogy—Philip G. Altbach, Gail P. Kelly, Hugh G. Petrie, and Lois Weis (eds.)

Critical Perspectives on Early Childhood Education—Lois Weis, Philip G. Altbach, Gail P. Kelly, and Hugh G. Petrie (eds.)

Black Resistance in High School: Forging a Separatist Culture—R. Patrick Solomon

Emergent Issues in Education: Comparative Perspectives—Robert F. Arnove, Philip G. Altbach, and Gail P. Kelly (eds.)

Creating Community on College Campuses—Irving J. Spitzberg and Virginia V. Thorndike

Teaching Education Policy: Narratives, Stories, and Cases—Hendrick D. Gideonse (ed.)

Beyond Silenced Voices: Class, Race, and Gender in the United States Schools—Lois Weis and Michelle Fine (eds.)

Troubled Times for American Higher Education: The 1990s and Beyond—Clark Kerr (ed.)

Higher Education Cannot Escape History: Issues for the Twenty-first Century—Clark Kerr (ed.)

The Cold War and Academic Governance: The Lattimore Case at Johns Hopkins—Lionel S. Lewis (ed.)

Multiculturalism and Education: Diversity and Its Impact on Schools and Society—Thomas J. LaBelle and Christopher R. Ward (eds.)

The Contradictory College: The Conflicting Origins, Impacts, and Futures of the Community College—Kevin J. Dougherty (ed.)

Race and Educational Reform in the American Metropolis: A Study of School Decentralization—Dan A. Lewis (ed.)

Professionalization, Partnership, and Power: Building Professional Development Schools—Hugh Petrie (ed.)

Ethnic Studies and Multiculturalism—Thomas J. LaBelle and Christopher R. Ward

Promotion and Tenure: Community and Socialization in Academe—William G. Tierney and Estela Mara Bensimon (eds.)

Sailing Against the Wind: African Americans and Women in U.S. Education—Kofi Lomotey (ed.)

The Challenge of Eastern Asian Education: Implications for America—William K. Cummings and Philip G. Altbach (eds.)

Conversations with Educational Leaders: Contemporary Viewpoints on Education in America—Anne Tumbau-Lockwood

Managed Professionals: Unionized Faculty and Restructuring Academic Labor—Gary Rhoades

The Curriculum, Second Edition—Landon E. Beyer and Michael W. Apple (eds.)

Education/Technology/Power: Educational Computing as a Social Practice—Hank Bromley and Michael W. Apple

Capitalizing Knowledge—Henry Etzkowitz, Andrew Webster, and Pat Healey (eds.)

The Academic Kitchen—Maresi Nerad